CROQUET

CROQUET

The Gentle but Wicket Game

Christopher R. Reaske

E. P. DUTTON  NEW YORK

Published in the United States by E. P. Dutton,
a division of NAL Penguin Inc.,
2 Park Avenue, New York, N.Y. 10016.

Published simultaneously in Canada by
Fitzhenry and Whiteside, Limited, Toronto.

Library of Congress Cataloging-in-Publication Data
Reaske, Christopher Russell.
Croquet : the gentle but wicket game.

1. Croquet.   I. Title.
GV931.R34   1988   796.35′4   87-35702
ISBN: 0-525-48385-3

DESIGNED BY EARL TIDWELL

1 3 5 7 9 10 8 6 4 2

First Edition

Grateful acknowledgment is given for permission
to quote from the following work:

A Rush on the Ultimate by H. F. R. Keating.
Copyright © 1961 by H. F. R. Keating.
Reprinted by permission of Doubleday and Co., Inc.

For my wonderful parents,

Alice I. R. Reaske
and
Herbert E. Reaske
(1907–1987)

Though't be a sportful Combate,
Yet in this triall
Much opinion dwells.
—WILLIAM SHAKESPEARE,
Troilus and Cressida

In war there is no second prize
for the runner-up.
—GENERAL OMAR BRADLEY

Contents

Contents

O

Preface

The greatest thing of all about croquet is that it is easy to learn and fun for people of all ages to play. Although to some the game has a lingering "elitist" image, in reality it is one of the most democratic games there is, open to all people everywhere. To have a ball playing croquet, you do not need to be to the mallet born. In this book I have pointedly staked out the position that *all* of the different "versions" of croquet are enjoyable and have their merits and challenges.

Anyone who enjoys playing croquet and then decides to write about it inevitably wants to see what other croquet players have had to say. As I am still slowly but menacingly improving my own croquet skills, I have consulted a number of technical books and reference works. Four have been particularly helpful: James Charlton and William Thompson, *Croquet* (New York, 1977); Jack Osborn and Jesse Kornbluth, *Winning Croquet: From Backyard to Greensward* (New York,

1983); Xandra Kayden, *The Basics of Croquet* (Cambridge, Mass., 1986); and David Park Curry, *Winslow Homer: The Croquet Game* (New Haven, 1984). The first three are invaluable with regard to rules, shots, and techniques, while the latter is the best sociological/historical account of the game I have discovered. A variety of other articles, magazines, portions of books, and tips from friends, librarians, and fellow croquet players have all benefited my writing.

O

Acknowledgments

I am particularly indebted, as always, to the wit of my wife, Mary K., who not only indulged my puns along the way but came up with some of her own, including the wonderful chapter title "With Mallet Aforethought" for the discussion of shots and strategies.

My agents, Martha Goldstein and Paul Bradley, have been helpful and supportive, and Kathy Hall again assisted me by preparing the final manuscript. Above all, I thank my editor at Dutton, Jeanne Martinet; her enthusiasm has been constant, her humor inspiring, her advice sound, and her editing and judgment superb. That she *flaunts* an old croquet ball—salvaged from its existence as a "closet" ball from her childhood home—in plain sight on her desk is more than sufficient testimony to her commitment as an editor.

Acknowledgments for artwork accompany the illustrations, but I would particularly like to thank my daughter, Suzanne, for providing the line illustrations.

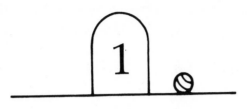

The Gentle
but
Wicket Game

You will know that you have a well-developed love of the great game of croquet the first time you ask your guests to move their cars and aim their headlights out onto the croquet lawn so that you can finish the game. You may have had too much to eat or drink, and the last light of the setting sun may now also have departed, along with the more rational side of your nature, but you will still have your eye menacingly fixed on Fred's ball and you know, if you know anything, that you will not be able to sleep if you don't hit it and thereby win the opportunity to send it to the other end of the lawn. This, after all, is what Fred did to your ball just a little while ago.

You don't *care* that Fred's ball will be placed back onto the lawn. You just want to hit it as hard and as far as you can—out of the yard, into the raspberry patch, down the road, *anywhere*, but at least as far as kingdom come. You hope Fred feels the pain. In fact, you hope it

Americans throughout this century have enjoyed "sending" an opponent's ball, in between drinks, in their backyards. "Croquet on the Lawn," 1940s illustration by Haddon Sundblom. *Courtesy: New York Public Library Picture Collection.*

hurts Fred as much as if a pin had been stuck in a voodoo doll of Fred. You hope that as he watches his ball disappear Fred mutters "shit" and that his wife *hears* it. In fact, you hope his wife now finds *you* more attractive than Fred. No matter what, Fred just can't be allowed to go home without getting a good taste of how it feels. And to think, you and Fred are good friends. And this, *my* friends, is when you will know that you love the "gentle but wicket" game of croquet.

Although croquet has come of age in the last twenty-five years and is now a fully regulated competitive sport, happily for us, it still endures as a late-afternoon and after-dinner recreation possessed of a mystique that has yet to be fully understood. Mystique aside, however, it is a game that is easy to learn to play, as more and more people are discovering.

There is something about croquet that brings out the beast in many of us. It sometimes leads to outrageous behavior, rudeness, and bald, uncurtailed aggression. It allows us to excuse the least civil parts of our nature. It can punish our smugness, spur us into conventional warfare, and even make us feel persecuted. Harpo Marx wrote of his crazy, joyful hours of croquet during the 1950s with a whole set of croquet fanatics, most of whom, as he noted, quickly became "croquemaniacs." Today the mania is spreading. Over 300,000 new croquet sets were sold in the last year in this country alone. Many cities, from Phoenix, Arizona, to Lexington, Kentucky, are building or thinking about building public croquet courts. *Newsweek* has recently heralded the "comeback" of croquet. So has *Town and Country*.

Croquet has actually had *many* widely recognized "comebacks" over the last six centuries. It is one of our more curious games in that the depth of its attractiveness seems hard to account for by even the most penetrating analysis of the elements of the game. Standing around doing *nothing* for much of the game (except, at times, thinking about what a pain in the ass Fred can be), you *have* to wonder why you love it so much. The game requires skill, of course, yet it is not the skill of an alpine skier that requires years and years to develop. Very young children enjoy playing croquet. The maiden issue of the magazine *Croquet Today* (Summer 1987) contained advice for three- and four-year-olds. "Seniors" enjoy playing too. The game requires a degree of thoughtfulness, of foxlike cunning, and yet so do many other games that have never enjoyed the long life and incredible "staying power" of croquet, which is now not only played in backyards around the world but in croquet clubs all over the United States, from Phoenix to New Haven (where members of the Yale Elizabethan Club sometimes don tuxedos before picking up their mallets), from Palm Beach

O

to Honolulu, from San Francisco to Southampton, from Grosse Point to Oklahoma City.

By every conceivable measure, whether sales of croquet sets, numbers of new clubs opening (there are some 250 clubs in the United States today, compared with 5 just a decade ago), or uses of croquet as a marketing image for other products, the popularity of the game is growing at an accelerating speed. On a recent day in New York, for example, I found three window displays for clothing that featured, in one instance, men's belts, shoes, hats, and trousers slung over croquet mallet stands and wickets, and, in another, the latest women's summer clothes hung on models playing croquet. At Brooks Brothers on Madison Avenue, wickets and stakes are sometimes displayed under glass with clothing. Revlon and Nikon are using croquet to market their wares. Smith College is currently installing a new croquet court, and others are expected to appear on campus soon. And while Yale and Harvard do not (yet) have their own courts, their eighth match took place in November 1987. No matter how you look at it, croquet is not simply in, it is taking control.

Like everything else in life, of course, croquet can be taken too seriously. Fred can be that way about it. Also about eating enough *fiber*. Fred's into both competitiveness *and* longevity. You know him! For some people croquet becomes the repository of virtually all ego gratification, and winning a croquet game becomes more important than everything else in life. People don't get like this about badminton and horseshoes. Croquet makes people crazy. Sometimes insanely jealous. Often menacingly near to "losing it." Such is the "fun" of the game. And there are, undoubtedly, those who take up croquet because it has been perceived as a game for the rich, the powerful, and the famous. Truth is, though, you don't need to be *anything* except willing and interested to take up the game.

The majority of croquet players take it up for social enjoyment and begin by enthusiastically playing the so-called basic "backyard" game of croquet. Although some feel this basic and most popular game is artlessly maligned as the plain Jane of the species, the game, like all variants, is fully ingenious: It allows us to civilize our aggres-

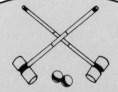

FIRST COLLEGE
CROQUET COURT:
SMITH COLLEGE, 1987

In the summer of 1987 *The New York Times* announced that for the first time in the United States, a college would create an official croquet court. Smith College's new court, resulting from special donated funds (and more would be welcome!), was the brainchild of English Professor Emeritus Richard Young, who described himself to me as an avid croquet enthusiast. He has been actively supportive of the New England Collegiate Croquet Association and proposed the idea to Smith College's president, who was quick to get behind the idea.

The court was designed to be of official tournament quality, with correct drainage and so forth, with an initial budget estimate of $16,000. It was first played on sometime during the summer of 1987, and certainly before the snow fell (as it occasionally has on the Yale–Harvard croquet game that precedes the now over one-hundred-year-old football rivalry). Interestingly enough, the support for the new croquet court, while largely coming from Smith College alumnae and friends, was also provided by several Vassar-related donors, so perhaps their enthusiasm for the game will bring Vassar a court before too long. In any case, given the game's increasing popularity, it is likely that other colleges will follow suit soon (incidentally, the New England Collegiate Croquet Association, or NECCA, is located in Cambridge, Massachusetts).

sion and hit, pursue, stalk, even *kill* one another all in the name of good fun. It doesn't take long, in any case, to become more than a little nuts about the game . . . or to risk ruining a friendship or two.

The basic backyard game of croquet has nine wickets and two stakes, is very challenging, and is *still* played happily on comfortably imperfect lawns at all hours of the day with a croquet set that may cost anywhere from under $50 to over $200. Some old sets may be had at garage sales for $3!

Then there is the rapidly emerging popular six-wicket croquet game played by more and more Americans and endorsed by the relatively recently formed (1977) United States Croquet Association. The USCA has played a very helpful, much needed, and important role in refining and standardizing the basic rules of croquet as played with six wickets and two stakes and with equipment having prices all over the map. Virtually all major competition and international tournament play centers on this six-wicket layout. The British game (also six wickets) has its ardent devotees. But the story does not end here.

In the fall of 1986 yet another American croquet association was formed, primarily to advocate and lobby for a different variety of six-wicket croquet. This group, known as the American Croquet Association (ACA), prefers what is known as the international form of croquet, with some differences from the game as played under the auspices of the USCA. And beyond all of this is, of course, a host of still other smaller groups and lobbying efforts that advocate this or that variation on one or more rules or theories. There is a monsoonlike quality to the literature and politics of croquet—with the wind blowing one way for one season and the other in the next. You can get into croquet to whatever level you want, even to the point of shelling out megabucks for an outfit that might include white-framed sunglasses, Chinese riding pants, and a designer cotton twill double-breasted coatdress (see p. 129).

I have chosen to write this book as an introduction to croquet for *all* actual and potential croquet players, and for both beginning and experienced players, not because I shy from controversy or deny the socioeconomic layering of our society (I play in denim shorts and sometimes barefoot . . . a barbarian notion in a Napa Valley tournament or on a court in Palm Springs or East Hampton), but because I honestly believe the game of croquet, like our own human species, is very much in a state of evolution.

Croquet, perhaps surprisingly, is a point of reference for social change, and its current revival is, in all likelihood, both a reflection and harbinger of change. The history of croquet, as summarized in the next chapter, is clearly an *unfinished* history. The basic game has been around for over six hundred years—a lot longer than cricket, stoop ball, baseball, and other bat-and-ball games—in various forms, all of which are and have been very easy to learn to play, and most of which will assuredly be around for at least that many more years and undoubtedly in new variations. It's a game with nostalgic, even atavistic, underpinnings, and its future is not controlled by anyone or by any one association. Wear nothing but a white placard-front Swiss cotton shirt if you feel like it. Go barefoot if you want to. Who's to tell?

The point is that croquet is a wonderful, upbeat game for both sexes and all ages and is growing in popularity despite the "politics" of different groups: East Coast and West Coast, competing associations, differences on both sides of the Atlantic, with subgroups around the world. If you think of croquet as a *sport* with different versions (games) to be played, it helps. Just as we play "poker," we also play stud poker, we play deuces and one-eyed jacks wild, and so forth. The different varieties of croquet have much more in common than they have that is different.

Croquet is a game whose very nature cries out for interpretation. It has been, at different times, the exclusive property of the elite upper crust (therefore considered a "power game" just as a pink tie with blue polka dots has been regarded as a "power tie") as well as *the* egalitarian game that can be played by members of both sexes and by people of all ages. Some devotees rhapsodize over the intellectuality of the game, the mathematical understanding required to hit one ball that hits another ball in such a way as to make them both go exactly where you want.

There has also been, at various times, a much-publicized fear-

O

fulness about croquet's moral impact. The fact that the game lends itself to open-air "mixed company" interaction and allows participants to examine one another in a variety of physical positions has caused not a little consternation at different times (see chapter 7). In any event, the broad American public appetite for croquet is now a well-established Main Street affair.

In some people's minds croquet is a quaint and literally gentle Victorian game in which good sportsmanship and polite manners carry the day. Yet to anyone who has played the game often, the inaccuracy of this image is as close at hand as your favorite mallet. More often than not during the course of a "gentle" game of croquet, it takes enormous restraint simply to keep yourself from hitting someone over the head. Croquet makes you grind your teeth, wrinkle your face, breathe hard, and perspire. Croquet has the ability to awaken every nerve in your body. Like a ball behind a wicket, you can easily become "wired." You have to sit or stand quietly while somebody literally treats your ball, and therefore you (make no mistake: When you play croquet, you *are* the ball), in incredibly shabby, mean, spiteful, sometimes insulting, and sometimes even inexplicably nasty ways. All you can do is *wait your turn.*

It is for this reason that croquet can perhaps best be understood as a game of vengeance. To the greater English population in the days of the first Queen Elizabeth, the most popular form of entertainment was seeing a revenge tragedy like Shakespeare's *Hamlet.* Today we see one movie after another, often a whole string of movies with the same central character, built around the theme of vengeance. Croquet is fantastic in that, unlike Western movies, for example, it allows you not simply to sublimate your desire to "get even" with someone but actually to do it. You can choose to play as aggressively as you want. You can hit somebody, stalk him, block him from getting ahead, isolate him, ostracize him, possibly destroy him, and, in one variation, even *poison* him. All you have to do is *wait your turn.*

In Lewis Carroll's *Alice in Wonderland* there is a wonderful chapter devoted to a game of croquet on the queen's croquet lawn. The images of flamingos turned upside-down for mallets and hedgehogs being used for croquet balls illustrate a kind of zaniness that is inherent to croquet. We could do with more zaniness in our world. *Zanni* is the Italian word for a masked clown, a mimic, an entertainer. Croquet can bring a little of that playful and light quality into our lives. And in the United States right now, no outdoor activity seems to be moving into vogue more rapidly.

○

Our contemporary society has created a megabusiness of aerobic sports, such as running and biking. Still, there is nothing wild or zany about running. Being in a triathlon doesn't bring any laughs. Our society is trying to come to grips with a new kind of leisure syndrome. We have more time, we live longer, and we have more money. But it seems to be growing clearer that we cannot aim *all* of this at the health clubs, fitness clubs, gyms, weights, marathons, and road races. The other side of the coin is increasingly represented by true leisure sports; and such lawn games as golf, bocce, badminton, and croquet are, if anything, likely to continue growing in popularity, not simply because they form a contrast to the tougher, more demanding kinds of "real" exercise, but because they provide for social interaction and zaniness. One thing is certain: The game inspires zealous followers, such as Chief Justice William Rehnquist or Averell Harriman, who as ambassador to Russia insisted that the Soviets establish a croquet lawn for his use. Harriman once held up the work of the New York State legislature for twenty minutes when he refused to break his concentration in a croquet game. Harpo Marx almost succeeded in installing an artificial-turf croquet lawn on top of his apartment building in New York but was, finally, thwarted by a city code and a fire marshal.

Croquet allows us to go nuts, crazy, or otherwise "off the ranch" without doing much harm to ourselves or to anyone else. Of course, if we play into the darkness too long, we may have dead car batteries, and then our excesses may be called into question. One should remember that in the eighteenth century the word "enthusiast" was often used simply to describe an insane person. That's a tad beyond a *zanni*.

If one good thing about croquet is that it can be wild, woolly, and wonderful, another is that the game has a uniquely entertaining language of its own. From wickets to hoops, stakes and mallets, breaks, splits, rushes, and cannon shots, it is fun to become fully conversant with croquet terminology. I believe, however, that you can explain how to play croquet—the rules, the strategies, and the techniques—without getting overly caught up in that special (at times riotously literal) language. To the greatest extent possible, I try to keep my language direct and accessible, while at the same time offering a full understanding of the basic language of the game (much of the terminology is recaptured for convenient reference in the glossary). Certainly you do not need to worry about using the "correct" language for everything you do on the croquet court. As often as not you will be talking the way you do naturally, presumably with a touch of implied violence: "It's my shot"; "I'm going to kill you"; "Did I hit her yet?"; "I made it through the wicket"; and so forth.

While the special language of croquet will emerge in succeeding chapters, I want to make one linguistic disclaimer right at the outset. Because croquet is a game of going through wickets, many people think that the phrase "sticky wicket" has its origins in croquet. It doesn't. A "sticky wicket"—often used colloquially to describe a tricky situation and sometimes now used to describe a croquet ball that is partway through a wicket—is in fact a description of a wet "wicket," or a group of two or three stakes in the English game of cricket. We *do* worry about getting "wicketed" in croquet, meaning having our ball caught in the middle of the wicket. And because one of my overarching (sic) concerns in writing this book is to keep you from being wicketed, I thought you should know the truth.

It cannot be emphasized too strongly that the language of croquet is worth knowing to the extent that *you* feel it is worth knowing, and to the extent that you can use it artfully to intimidate your opponent. You can usually make yourself understood in a croquet game without using any new words, including "croquet" itself. Four-letter words, in fact, are muttered as frequently in croquet as in any other competitive sport. You don't need to describe what you are doing to anyone. What matters is that you know *what* you are doing. After a

She's looking at the ball and he's looking at her. However, her ankle is probably not going to see daylight, so he might as well regard the ball. An 1875 English illustration from *Cassell's Household Guide. Courtesy: New York Public Library Picture Collection.*

few drinks, you may even be found asking such fundamentally more important questions as which *is* your ball, which *side* of the wicket you are supposed to go through this time, and so forth. All of which is fine, as the game is meant to be enjoyed, zany, and filled with quasi-lustful adventure, rhythms of flirtation and courtship, and even a sense of comedy. If at a certain point in history critics of the game worried about women's skirts rising in various ways on various strokes, what might they think today when someone who is really tanked up (say near the end of a long game) plays as if it were horseless polo?

To a rapidly growing number of Americans, croquet is becoming as standard a part of backyard culture as barbecuing hamburgers and hot dogs. You may build a fire on the gravel in the driveway or you may use a Weber, but you can enjoy the food either way. So it is with the various levels of sophistication on which croquet can be enjoyed. Croquet is now firmly established as a part of our emerging leisure lifestyle. For one thing, although there are, happily, increasing numbers of "seniors" playing softball and tennis, there are also many more who can enjoy a less knee-threatening game like croquet. The 1987 *Newsweek* article, in fact, pointed out that the year's top players were seventy-one. Incidentally, about one-third of the increase in our longevity as a species from the earliest prehistoric times has been made since 1900. We have a long life ahead of us, and croquet will be as much a part of our lengthening future as it has been of our past. It is and it is not a "gentle" game. It is in that it can, in theory, be played in very civil ways. It is *not* in that it tends to draw out some of our less civilized impulses, thereby satisfying our basic need not only for aggression but for the deeper "reward" feelings that come only from true vengeance.

While we are now far beyond debating the morality of the game and instead caught up in new—and yes, at times downright silly—debates about the height of the grass in tournament play, placement of balls, and the advantages of different varieties of the game, surely it is clear that much of croquet's romance lies in its very instability or, stated differently, in its ability to appeal to our most basic instincts and intelligence in some unusually powerful way. The game has provoked controversy because it is a provocative game, a tease, a challenge. Certainly it defies being "finalized" as a species just as much as we do.

In this book I provide a complete guide to the different games of croquet, explain how to play them—the basic rules and protocol—and outline the strategies and shots one can easily learn and use in any version of the game. I try to provide the reader with a sense of the satisfaction that comes from playing croquet skillfully and competitively, but always with the underlying assumption that a croquet court, while admittedly a major world battlefield, should not, in any final appraisal, be mistaken for reality. I am a writer and a croquet fan, and I believe that croquet is a game inherently tied to fantasy and that this is as "proper" as some mistakenly suppose the gentle game to be. Before turning to the basics of croquet, it is fun to reflect on just a bit of the unfinished history of the game. Its voyage in the world thus far provides a window into its essentially cosmopolitan nature.

The Gentle but Wicket Game

○

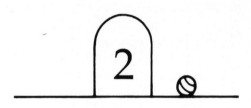

Croquet: An Unfinished History

Croquet's ancestry is distinctively international, drawing on elements, manners, and even character traits from France, Ireland, England, and other countries. That the game has grown in popularity throughout the ages and is even played regularly in such distant locales as Australia and Singapore is evidence of its irresistible appeal and character. The story of croquet's evolution is colorful, and while marred slightly by those who have—to our contemporary astonishment—found it too sexual in its nature for men and women to play together, or by those unable to agree on its rules, its history is nevertheless dynamic and a good foreshadowing of what lies ahead.

Displays of fierce emotion, sometimes referred to as histrionics, are more familiar to us when thinking about croquet than the game's actual history. This should not come as a surprise. A lot of us don't know much about our parents' childhood (sometimes not even our own), so why should we know anything about a game's? Mostly, I

Throughout history croquet has inspired any number of furtive glances. Detail of seventeenth century Flemish tapestry, from Kozel Castle, Czechoslovakia.

suppose, because it reminds us that while Americans are now going crazy over the game, so are and have people in different parts of the world for six centuries. We're but part of a story that is, as George Santayana once said of science, "far from final." While today people debate the merits of tennis-court-like sand croquet courts (in South Australia) as opposed to croquet courts laid down on synthetic grass, in times past similarly intense debates centered on such issues as whether the game might further the decline of alcoholics and whether the wickets should be wider or narrower.

To understand croquet as a very dynamic evolving sport with an "unfinished" history, one need only briefly consider its voyage thus far.

Although some who tend to see more socialite than savage in

15

While the croquet players here are intent on what they are doing, the spectators don't seem to care much. Even the sheep seem a little uninterested, despite the presumably lively pace of the game as it was played four hundred years ago. Sixteenth-century French tapestry. *Courtesy: Collection Fenaille.*

croquet cannot easily believe it, the game really does appear to have evolved from a game first played by, yes, *peasants* (shudder) in France in the thirteenth century. This game, known as *paille maille* (= pell mell = *palla mallens,* the Latin for ball and mallet), seems to have begun as a game using mallets to knock balls through "hoops" (oversized, more rounded, much wider wickets) to hit a peg on the other side. By the sixteenth century pell mell was being played in England and slowly being transformed into the more complicated game of croquet—more complicated because players had to pass their balls through wickets (or hoops, as they continue to be called in England) in a particular order and because the balls got bigger and the wickets got smaller. Pell mell became known as pall mall and was played regularly and with great zeal on the area now named the Pall Mall in London.

This transition to bigger balls needing to go through smaller wickets marks the early sense of perversity that has not left the game. The change well represents the vexing, at times irritating, nature of the game. Just when you think you are doing things pretty well, getting if not the hang at least the swing of it, some aspect of the game changes: The weight of the balls, the number of wickets, the placement of the stake. Though some may ask, "Why can't anyone leave it all alone?" it appears the game may forever be developing. Undoubtedly the day will come when the height of the wicket is lowered (this is not quite like lowering the boom) and we will have to go through yet another agonizing change. Croquet hates permanency.

By 1852 the first croquet "instruments" as we know them today were being made in London, and the game had already been embraced for about twenty years in Ireland. According to various versions of the legends, croquet was introduced into England by an Englishman who had been given a set of equipment by an Irish lady friend in about 1840. Before long it had reached the hands of a French toymaker and manufacturer, John Jacques, who began mass production of croquet equipment, which rapidly flooded England. Given its French beginnings (those peasants, I gather, were in the *south* of France, which seems to irritate even further those who would prefer

Sitting or standing, playing or waiting to play, croquet is about as unaerobic as a sport can be. Victorian photograph.

a more aristocratic conception), Jacques's role seems not only fortuitous but appropriate.

As croquet mushroomed in its popularity into one of the leading pastimes of the English leisure class, it suddenly was again being rediscovered and taken up no less enthusiastically in France. In England the enthusiasm was particularly sharp among women who felt that they had finally been given a game they could play as equals with men. It is hard to be certain just what the male-female mix was when the game was first beginning in France, but clearly in England the women could not be restrained in their relish for the game—and clearly, too, the men had no interest in restraining them.

Croquet was so popular that it was as if Michael Jackson had exploded onto the scene. (Today Fred likes to think he has a similar impact when he arrives, filled with fiber, at a croquet match.) In England in the 1850s women were playing croquet at every opportunity. Typical of the game's growing popularity is the statement from

"The workmen have come out . . . to mow the lawn into perfect smoothness, and make it as even as we trust the paths of the players may be through life" (*Harper's Weekly*, 1871). Croquet's interaction with moral behavior has been a focus of commentary for over a hundred years.

the English magazine *Field* in 1858: "There is no game which has made such rapid stride in this county [Meath] within a few years as croquet."

Across the Atlantic the enthusiasm was also beginning to take hold, though perhaps with less of the frenzied excitement. Consider, for example, this passage from Louisa May Alcott's *Little Women*, published in 1868; clearly there is less élan in this description of what might be summarized as a rather sedating encounter: "Little Jo was through the last wicket, and had missed the stake . . . Fred . . . gave a stroke, his ball hit the wicket, and stopped an inch on the wrong side." That may go down as one of the great nonevents captured in American literature! Imagine being off by a full inch! Of course you would go out of your gourd with joy if *your* "friend" Fred made such a dippy shot, especially if his wife said she hoped he would soon "catch up."

By the 1870s the game had become particularly popular in a few

19

American spots such as Norwich, Connecticut, but soon it was being played up and down the East Coast and slowly expanding to other locales. One person has recalled his family's playing croquet on the hotel grounds at the Springs in Clarendon Spa on July 4, 1882. Although lawn tennis had entered the United States at about the same time, croquet was vastly more popular for the last quarter of the nineteenth century. It is hard to say why. Was it because, unlike croquet, tennis required more physical exertion? Or, was it because the rules for tennis were standardized world-wide, and it was therefore less controversial? In any case, by the turn of the century on both sides of the Atlantic, and perhaps partly due to growing changes in the English societal makeup (certainly once the land tax laws were reformed and a greater number of people in England had to do more than keep track of their income from capital), croquet, and leisure time as well, went into a decline.

One should probably bear in mind that the whole concept of summer vacations didn't take hold in the United States until the middle of the nineteenth century. Railroads made it easier for people to get out in the country and take up such outdoor sports as tennis, golf, and croquet.

While in the early years of the twentieth century many people, including Mark Twain and Calvin Coolidge, typically went off to play croquet at country estates such as those at Saranac Lake in upstate New York, by the time the market crashed, the game was temporarily a bit less in the limelight.

Some social historians theorize that the decline was attributable to the drinking excesses that frequently accompanied the game, and when a war was on, the riotous, less responsible activity associated with croquet made it even less attractive. In the 1930s and forties the popularity of croquet burgeoned and grew steadily. That many Hollywood stars were also avidly playing croquet contributed in no small way to the general public's new appetite for the game.

It was also during this period that croquet increasingly became perceived as a wonderful kind of war game. The outrageous, wild, and sometimes drunken style of play exhibited by movie stars such

If having F. Scott Fitzgerald on the cover couldn't sell the magazine, croquet could—with the talents of Norman Rockwell. *Saturday Evening Post* cover © 1931 The Curtis Publishing Company. *Courtesy: Norman Rockwell Estate.*

as Harpo Marx led more than a few Americans to begin playing without inhibition. Laying out courts in new and exotic ways became fashionable—not unlike some of the zany backyard layouts that some people create today when they feel like changing the game. Typical of the growing mania of this kind of unabashed warriorlike game is one in fact well described by Harpo in his autobiography *Harpo Speaks*. He writes that he and a group of his friends:

o

> once spent a wonderful weekend at Otto H. Kahn's estate. The minute we arrived there we started to play croquet, without bothering first to pay our respects to our host. Kahn's course was as flat and smooth as a billiard table. It was more like a golf green than a croquet court, which gave me an idea. I started experimenting with a golf-type swing, using the mallet like a mashie. The other three gleefully joined in the experiment, and the croquet balls went zooming all over the place. Garden furniture got knocked over. Greenhouse windows were smashed. Servants ran the gauntlet from main house to guesthouse with arms clutched over their heads. Kahn himself fled to his yacht, which was anchored in the Sound at the foot of the lawn, and hoisted a white flag. He didn't emerge from the yacht until nightfall, when the world was once again safe from croquemaniacs.

Over the years there have been formed a number of croquet clubs and associations—formed, but then re-formed, disbanded, reunited, and endlessly worried about. The first known croquet club was established in 1865, in Worthing, England. (The first croquet tournament was held at Evesham, England, August 15–16, 1867.) A faction later split off to form the National Croquet Club, and so it has gone over the years, with the recent division in the United States—where people are *supposed* to take all of this a little more gingerly—into croquet associations with differing objectives, theories, and game preferences. What is most intriguing about all of this lies not in the specifics, however, but in the general patterns of dissent and compromise. Croquet refuses to be dominated by any one group, person, or "faction." In *Alice in Wonderland* Alice noted that nobody seemed

MALLET'S LITERARY FAME

Be aware of a famous mallet. Specifically, one David Mallet (1705–1765), who collaborated with J. Thomson (1700–1748) to write and produce the English masque *Alfred*, which, it turns out, includes the famous song "Rule Britannia." Mallet was the literary executor of Henry St. John Bolingbroke.

to be able to agree about the rules. The game *is*, at times, contentious, and inspires both great passions and moments of petulance. That people develop such strong feelings about the game to the point of association politics is therefore not surprising. And there will be further developments, of that we can all be certain. You can stake your life on it.

Before leaving the history of the game, consider the historical side of just a bit of the game's language. "Hoops" (now a common name for scruffy games of basketball) are not only the early name for the arched wickets but refer to the semicircular parts of women's petticoats and the curved metal used for casks. "Wickets" have always been considered archways to pass through. One can even find Milton, in *Paradise Lost*, writing "Now Saint Peter / At Heav'ns Wicket seems to wait them / With his keys." Of course, to a croquet enthusiast, the idea of entering heaven through a wicket has no equally attractive image. "Wicket" has also been used colloquially and interchangeably with "wicked," as in "It's a wicket night out." And "wicked/wicket" means "terrific" in popular usage, which is why croquet is wicket as well as gentle, particularly in Locust Valley.

"Mallet" comes from the French word *maillet*, or wooden ham-

A private game of croquet on the Isle of Wight, 1865. *Courtesy: New York Public Library Picture Collection.*

mer, and was called a mall in England, so that in 1662 we find the rule "That noe persons shall after play carry their malls out of St. James's Parke without leave of the said keeper." (*Mauling* Fred with your mallet, however, has occurred to you more than once.) So malls or *mailles* or mallets were as carefully guarded then as they were when Harpo Marx designed a special climate-controlled room in his New York apartment for his mallets, to keep them from splitting. He also took a few showgirls—who were determined to advance their careers by not leaving his party when it was over—into this croquet equipment room and scared them away by running his hands up and down the shaft of one of the mallets, saying that he had some strange things he would like to do with them. Their malletaise was such that they didn't stay around to see what he might have had in mind! For fellow seafood enthusiasts, note that the mallet-headed oyster of the genus *Malleus,* yet to be eaten by this writer, is now on the lengthening list of "before I dies." Come to think of it, "mallet-headed" might make an appropriate insult.

"Croquet" itself is a French word rooted in the dialects of northern France as a form of *crochet* or *croc* or *croche*, meaning "shepherd's crook" and undoubtedly reflecting the shape of the early mallets. Today in France these words still refer to a hockey stick. This derivation also explains why the game was called "crooky" in Ireland, which the British with their usual historical rivalry enjoyed satirizing as "croaky."

The French, the Irish, the Americans . . . the language behind the game mirrors its international heritage. The game's appeal was carefully spread by way of toy manufacturers, producing croquet sets known as croqueterie (although as the *Newsweek* article on the tremendous recent "comeback" of croquet observed, those not in the know think of croqueterie as a chicken dish) accompanied by rule books. Magazine articles, photos, and postcards of people playing croquet also kept feeding the lawns. I recently came across (in an antique dealer's collection in Mackinaw City, Michigan) a wonderful early-twentieth-century penny postal showing men (and *only* men) playing on croquet grounds set up in Prospect Park, Brooklyn, New York. The card, manufactured in Germany, shows men well dressed in suits and bowler hats both playing and sitting on various types of lawn chairs. The writer of the postal begins by saying "Dear friend, Suppose you have played the game of 'croquet.' " The card was clearly sent to illustrate as well as spread the word about the game. And although world wars interrupted the game a bit and altered the boundaries of nations, the underlying force that croquet had now become, its mystique, continued unabated. Since the formation in 1867 of the New York Croquet Club, countless clubs have sprung up all over the country. Many are private and not particularly interested in publicity. Many more will emerge. The satisfaction of hitting Fred's ball, really hitting it, getting back at him, making him suffer, indeed humiliating him if possible, is no less than it ever was. Throughout the country more resorts are building croquet courts. In fact, hoteliers are discovering that hosting croquet tournaments is good business, and a number of states, including Vermont, are having discussions about how to co-host tournaments with liquor distributors. It's not

O

○

that the two need to go together, but it does make sense. And history has already forged a romance between the game and the desire to socialize with drinks.

But before you actually get out onto the croquet lawn with Fred, much less with Steve and Wendy, or their English cousin Harriet, and her fiancé, Charles (whom you will meet shortly), there are a few things you may want to know. Do you really need to think about what to wear, where to play, how to select a croquet set, what kind of lawn to strive to create? Well, yes and no, I suppose. *Some* pregame advice is necessary or, at least (I think), interesting, to have under your belt before you start playing the gentle but wicket game of croquet.

3

Preparing to Play: Mind-set and Croquet Set

Some who advise about preparing to play croquet tell you to roll the lawn flat, cut the grass, measure the court, place the wickets and stake(s), choose your colors, master the basic shots in some practice sessions, and then have at it. This is a generally sound approach except for one thing: It ignores the most fundamental aspect of preparing to play croquet—mind-set. Try to remember this cardinal rule: *Mind-set is more important than croquet set.* Cling to this principle more tightly than you grip your mallet. After all, Joan of Arc is not the only one to have been burned at the stake.

   Croquet is hardly physically active enough to pass for a "sport" in the first place. Some people—why, I don't know—assert that because the equipment has become heavier the game has become more rugged; even stronger iron wickets are sometimes discussed as if they were weight-room accessories. Pumping wickets? How many calories can you burn in a croquet game beyond those naturally used up by breathing? There is no aerobic capacity required, and surely there is no aerobic output (forget overloading with pasta or carbohydrates ahead of time). You don't move fast, not at any point in the game. You certainly don't move *far* as in golf, where you might at least walk a few miles (I have never understood why any but the physically handicapped ride in golf carts). In fact, in much of the game you don't *move* at all. More than one person has turned their mallet upside down and stuck it in the ground to improvise a chair. Making people stand in one place is an ancient torture practice. Of course, if it has been raining recently and the ground is soft and you have much weight at all, you can sink your mallet into the earth too far and risk getting hung up in any one of several embarrassing positions. But even *that* makes no cardiovascular demands.

Not only do you not move much, far, or quickly, you don't require any particular strength or fitness to do what little you do. Much of what you "do" is covered by the following: slow soft swings of a mallet and an occasional "action-packed" chopping stroke; bending over to lift or move your ball after hitting another ball; bending slightly at the knee from time to time. I can't think of anything else. There is no need to do stretch exercises, warm-ups, calisthenics, or literally anything physical to get ready to walk out on to the croquet lawn. No cool-down afterward either. Certainly a shower is not warranted. But getting into a winning *mind-set;* well, that is another matter—the critical matter.

If you want to enjoy a "good game of croquet," you obviously want to enjoy it only up to a point. After that you mostly want to win the game, enjoy defeating somebody else. Especially Fred. He is really such a pain in the ass. It feels good to win, but it can feel even better to prepare yourself mentally for winning. What does this entail?

First, you need to decide at what level of the game you want to begin the process of intimidation. You might, for example, want to select a top-of-the-line croquet set (it's easy to spend over a thousand dollars if you really want to go big) to make a statement about the

CROQUET SPEED

Our modern society pays a lot of attention to speed. Time is of great value. Thus it is ironic that a game as popular as croquet can be *so slow*.

I don't know whether anyone has ever timed the speed of a croquet ball's movement (I checked out *my* shots—they are *very* slow!), but it is generally pretty mild, nothing like sky-diving, for example, where a body typically free-falls at 185 mph, or like golf, where a ball coming off the tee has been timed electronically at almost the same speed, 170 mph. Of course, croquet is still not the complete turtle you might think. Granted, it is nonaerobic and, some would say, as slow as molasses; however, other sports get the clock down even further. Wrestling can be pretty slow; one wrestler may hold another in a position for hours (and embraces that last that long are not amorous). According to *The Guinness Book of World Records*, however, it's the *tug-of-war* that *really* can be slow. In a good "tug" in Jubbulpore, India, on August 12, 1889, the winners moved a total of twelve feet in two hours and forty-one minutes, to clock in at an undizzying speed of 0.00084 mph. I have to confess that when I went looking I thought I might find that croquet would be cited as one of the slowest sports around, but the tug-of-war was the real *sleeper!*

o

degree to which you are "into" the game. You perhaps have long ago passed through backyard croquet, nine-wicket croquet, and now are totally committed to *official* American six-wicket croquet. Rather than do a song and dance about this (you consider it growth; don't be sure others do), you simply buy a terrific set, pay someone (it used to be a teenager in the neighborhood but now it's Andy's Lawn Service and costs five times as much) to get your grass into decent shape, and maybe even buy a "deadness board." You don't have to use it, just display it prominently. All of this will make quite an impression on your guests. They will notice your accoutrements. They will take it all in. They will compare it to their own scruffy croquet set and more casually placed wickets. Most of them, though unfortunately not Fred, will feel intimidated.

There are other ways to achieve the same upper hand. Again, you have to think about your plan. Mind-set is everything. If mind-set is best served by having a certain kind of croquet set, fine, but mind-set still is the central focus. One way to intimidate, for example, is to spend a lot of time building up your forearms. Really get them up to vein-bulging proportions, maybe by pumping wickets some evenings when it's too dark to play. While croquet does not require strength, it does require skill, particularly with regard to your ability to exercise "tight" control over your shots, to swing your mallet with great precision. If your guests notice your blue-ridged, enlarged forearms, they will make some assumptions about your control, your ability to make clean and highly controlled shots. If they compare their own sticklike forearms to your engorged ones, they will probably go into the game on the defensive. So, if pumping iron will help, go for it.

Of course there is clothing. Like graffiti in a bathroom stall, it will be read, tasteless or not. You can go all the way into the whites, giving yourself a clinical glow and taking on the quasi-deified authority that we have come to invest in the medical profession. This might mean white slacks or skirt, white shirt or blouse, white sun visor (an awesome touch), white wrist sweatband (again, not because you could *ever* work up a sweat in a croquet game, but there

In its 1987 maiden issue, the new magazine *Croquet Today* made it clear in photographs such as this one that croquet is for everyone and that people should dress as comfortably as they like. *Courtesy:* Croquet Today.

is a warrior heritage in the armbands-to-wristbands move that will suggest strength), of *course* white footwear, and so forth. White has a purity and a traditional elegance and presence. Or you can Darth Vader it in menacing blacks (and sweat in the summer sun).

Another intimidating clothing choice is a very breezy free and open outfit that suggests you want maximum freedom of movement to exercise your shots. You want the opposition to read in your clothing a commitment to perfection. The point is to think about what you wear. Think about the impact it will have on the particular people you have invited to play. If you know they hate a certain color, wear it.

In addition to thinking about such external expressions as croquet sets, lawn status, and attire, mind-set preparation requires a Zen-like meditative pass-through set of exercises. You must believe in yourself. Do some breathing exercises. Expunge any stress. Close your eyes. Imagine you are a croquet ball. Take yourself through each wicket. *Count* the wickets several times. Count the stakes too. Focus on your breathing until you reach a free state and then slowly replace it with an incredibly strong kind of "centering" concentration that has as its purpose a plan to present a soft and friendly veneer over an iron will committed to victory. Plan your first words carefully. A good opener, for example, is to say people look tired and you hope they are feeling all right. You can even just ask "Is anything wrong?" Or you can do some jumping jacks in place (or dive to the ground and do a set of push-ups) as your opponents arrive and joke about getting ready for the match. This will distract them, confuse them. Why are you doing jumping jacks or push-ups? They won't know what to make of it.

Another good mind-set activity is to think of *why* you hate the opponents, what you particularly dislike about them. If you've played croquet with them several times, there is probably plenty you can't stand. If you do like them in some respects, try to block out those good feelings. You can get them back later, and much more naturally, especially if *you* win and they lose. Remember: This is not a time to be a "softie."

One particularly fruitful mind-set activity is to imagine terrible things happening to the opponents. Picture them being trapped by packs of wolves. Maybe even by Papa-werewolf Chuck Connors. Fantasize that they are drowning in an oily sea. Picture their clothes suddenly whipped off them by a sudden miniature tornado, leaving them frightened and vulnerable, covering themselves as best they can (a mallet and a ball won't go too far in this regard) as if being banished from Eden. By picturing their vulnerability and fearfulness in your mind's eye, you can begin to build a bridge toward the hoped-for outcome, which must *begin* as wishing for nothing less than their total defeat. You can lighten up a little bit later in the game. But start from this harsh and angry base. It will help immensely.

Also try to think of what the opponents may be doing to psych *you* out. Be suspicious of *every* word and sign. If Steve yawns or says he is tired, ignore it. If he says he's not sure he's "up" for the game, don't believe him. This pose of impotence is a classic opening gambit in any competitive situation. This guy has been "up" for not only this game but just about everything else. If Wendy says she's thinking of playing less croquet and more tennis, don't ask her why. Assume it's a ruse. Rather, study them carefully during the first few moments. If Wendy asks for lime and Perrier, look out! You know she is determined to win this time. If Steve asks if *he* can pour *you* a gin and tonic, don't let him. He'll make it stronger than you want. If someone comments on your clothing ("I just love that shirt, where did you find it?"), either pretend you didn't hear the question (and actually you didn't *find* it, you bought it) or instead ask one of them where he got *his* shirt because it's so much more appropriate. This, like jumping jacks, will confuse.

Repeat-time: Mind-set is more important than croquet set. Norman Vincent Peale made a fortune selling the power of positive thinking. Think like a winner. Crush the opponents psychologically before you begin to play. Recall a bad shot one of them made the last time you got together for a "good game of croquet." Say to Wendy, loudly and with a husky (almost sexual) chuckle, "Do you remember that *hilarious* time when *Steve* hit his ball off the lawn under the car?" Steve will love a question like that. The harder he laughs, the more you know you got to him.

Someone once remarked that when it comes to losing there are good sports and there are those who can't act very well. So be a good actor as you prepare to play. If acting superior is called for, adjust a wicket a centimeter—call much attention to this correction. If acting inferior is called for, recall one of your own (few) bad shots from another contest. Let the opponents think you are still aware of it. Don't reveal that it took months to process the stress associated with that bad shot. If the stress associations return, stare at the stake and repeat the names of the colors. This is an excellent method of reducing anxiety.

Now, while mind-set is all, there is nevertheless a need to set

o

up the course and do a *few* things before you play. First, obviously, you need to decide which version you will play and set up the wickets and stake(s) accordingly (see the diagrams illustrating the placement of wickets, stake, and the progressive course of the ball in chapter 4). I once was advised to place the stake "vertically." Maybe it would be fun to play a game with the stake lying down. You know, a low stakes game, just for the heck of it. Of course, you do have to acquire a croquet set of some kind, and here it is worth pausing to note a few basic differences.

You can purchase mallets of all kinds and at a variety of prices. Take a look at an issue of *Croquet* magazine or write to the USCA and request its list of croqueterie makers (don't show your ignorance by pricing the "extra crispy") and you will get a sense of what is available. In Sonoma, California, for example, Pendulum makes precision mallets out of Delrin and nylon. The Forster Company in Wilton, Maine, advertises that it has made more than half of all the croquet sets sold in the United States in recent years. Their new entry is a United States Croquet Association–approved croquet set that sells for approximately $220. Each set includes four hardwood mallets; the heads are made of northern rock maple, have brass-ferruled tips, and measure 2⅞ by 9 inches, and the handles are made of ash and measure 36 inches. These dimensions are standard, as are the 3⅝-inch balls of compressed wood with colored, catalyzed, epoxy finish. Nine white steel wickets, 18 inches high, are included, as are color-striped hardwood stakes. This set comes complete with individually colored marker clips, rules and instructions books, and a heavy-duty canvas carrying case. The balls weigh 14 ounces, and the wickets 12 ounces. I mention the details for those of you who may be unfamiliar with the precision with which croquet sets are now manufactured and described. So, is a mallet a mallet a mallet, or what?

Anyone can select a croquet set for backyard or tournament croquet. The point is to decide how often you intend to play, what sort of care you intend to invest in your set (if you plan to leave everything outdoors all summer, why get the best?), and what your real purposes are. It is logical to begin to play croquet with a basic backyard croquet

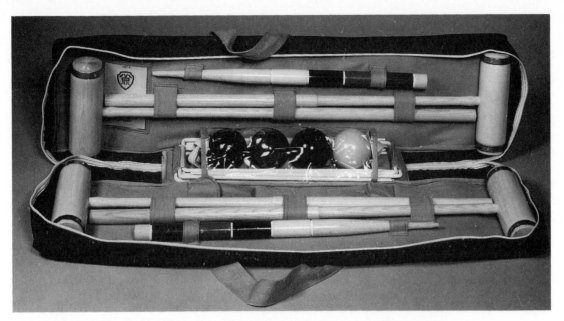

Forster's 4-Player Challenge "C" Class Croquet Set is very popular; it comes complete with rules and instructions books as well as a weather-resistant canvas carrying case.

set, and there are many available in stores throughout the country. Then, if and as you become a more serious player, you will naturally gravitate toward better, more durable equipment. Many companies market both a "family" set and a "tournament" set. Croquet sets are, frankly, more attractive as they become more expensive, and there *is* a new kind of satisfaction that comes into the game as your equipment improves (this is true of most sports), but top-of-the-line equipment is *not* necessary to the game. What kind of equipment to purchase, then, is really very subjective. If you are going to play official association croquet with six-pound cast-iron wickets, fine. But do you really need them for your yard and your occasional weekend game? Only you can decide.

Take croquet balls for a minute. There are rules governing the correctness of the balls in tournament play. A ball must bounce back

35

O

a certain minimum number of inches when dropped from a certain distance onto a hard surface (our relationships should have similar "resiliency" tests). This proof of regulation-required "elasticity," as it is called, is important in tournament play. But if you are at the average level of the game and play it primarily for the satisfaction of a good competition and an entertaining social life, you certainly are not going to spend any time at all bouncing balls around to see how they hold up.

What else? There is knowing what the rules are. This means reading either a book like this or one of the short rules books that typically come with croquet sets (*they*, however, do not typically address mind-set), or getting a friend (someone you trust!) to teach you. You may also write to the USCA and it will send you the rules. The only other thing you need to do is to get dressed. You don't have to *be* in shape to play croquet. What other sport lets you smoke and drink all the way through the game if you feel like it—bowling? You certainly don't have to "get into" shape either. If people of all shapes, sizes, and degrees of fitness can make love, well, I guess they surely can play croquet!

After a game of croquet, that's something else again. *You* shouldn't feel wiped out, but you can wipe off your mallet and hang it up carefully, you can rub loose blades of grass off each ball and rack them. You can clean the dirt off wickets and stakes (you may not want to be *observed* doing this), water the lawn, pick up any cigarette butts and dirty glasses. One could go on. But to prepare to play, well, if there is anything incremental left, it would have to be in one area and one area only: *attitude.*

Attitude differs from mind-set in that it stands for how you really *feel* toward a game of croquet in general and how you feel about a particular game you are about to play. And attitude can change if you want it to. For example, let's assume that you have been playing croquet for part of one summer. You have never won. You have trouble hitting another ball if it is more than three feet away. In short, your confidence is not that high.

Knowing all of this, however, you can still adopt a positive at-

This young girl looks like she has a very positive mind-set. Victorian sheet music cover. *Courtesy: The American Antiquarian Society.*

titude. Just make a determined effort in your mind, and the body will deliver. You need to say to yourself, "Okay, so I haven't been that hot when I've played the game before, but after all, I haven't been playing very long. I'm going to give it my best shot. For me, the real victory will be if I can play better than I have before." This strategy will allow you to compete with yourself, really, while you are of course competing with others. And if you are playing with a partner, tell him or her that you plan to do your best, that your skill is still developing, and frankly, that you will appreciate having some advice, particularly with regard to basics (Are you holding your mallet the best way? Are you swinging smoothly?). By adopting a positive attitude, you can augment the more deliberately strategic "mind-set" approach. Mind-set is, to some degree, necessarily self-induced, and so is attitude. Mind-set organizes your aggression against the opponent, however, and is aimed at figuring out how to "psych" him or her out. Attitude is your dialogue with yourself and/or a partner about your determination to play as well as *you* can.

Another point about attitude: Don't talk yourself into thinking it will be the end of the world if you play out of turn, hit the wrong ball, or hit a ball on which you are "dead" (see glossary). The odds are very great that you will be corrected by somebody, and usually *before* you actually do anything. Learning to play croquet is just that, learning. Everyone begins at some point, and while some people may become a bit nervous about the language of the game, and others about whether it is really a sport for everyone or just for the upper class, everyone needs to get over some kind of initial hurdle, and certainly nobody has any particular advantage due to height, weight, sex, age, or body type.

Mind-set involves making a decision in a very calculating way about how you are going to present yourself to the opposition, with a goal of intimidation, polite or otherwise. Attitude is a kind of quiet, honest contract you make with yourself about how you are going to play. Above all, don't let yourself think it will be "the end" if you lose. Somebody is going to lose the game. It is but one game out of several or more that you will, in all likelihood, be playing with the same people. You may even play with them many times over many years. So try to go into each game with an attitude of improving *your* skills and having a good time, win or lose. It helps, incidentally, to keep in mind Winston Churchill's notion that it is best to be optimistic because there does not seem to be much use being anything else!

O

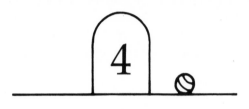

The Basic Games

There are a number of different "games" of croquet, and they are all easy to learn. However, each game has its own rules, procedures, wicket and stake layouts, court size, and even etiquette. It is easy to hit yourself in the foot if you don't know what you are doing.

My purpose in this chapter is not to argue "for" one kind of croquet over another. Nor do I wish to offer a litany of advantages and disadvantages. I simply wish to present clearly the basic information necessary to play each of the three principal and most popular games: 1) "nine-wicket croquet," played both informally as "backyard croquet" and more formally under rules of the United States Croquet Association; 2) American (six-wicket) croquet, also governed by official rules of the USCA; 3) "Association," or British, croquet (which also uses six wickets). Mentioned briefly is the related but far less frequently played game of roque.

I intend to discuss each game and to illustrate the way the principal rules operate as you and a few imaginary friends actually *play* the game. If in choosing this approach I have overlooked a minor rule or two, I feel confident that the tedium of a "1, 2, 3, 4, 5, 6" approach to the rules will have been avoided. And besides, most croquet sets include a listing of the rules. My goal is to make the game quickly accessible to everyone.

I have chosen to begin with the basic backyard game of croquet as it is played with nine wickets and two stakes because many people, and especially beginners, want to play it this way in their own yards. It is, furthermore, the croquet game that most adults remember from their childhood and also the one to which most people will be introduced. While nine-wicket croquet has evolved to the point that there are definite rules and regulations governing the game, backyard croquet by its very nature is less formal and precise. At least some of its appeal lies in what may be called its "toleration factor." Indeed, in some circles people playing backyard croquet are generally "forgiven" all kinds of things, from missed balls to being given opportunities to "take back" decisions, take shots over, and so forth. This game is unusually friendly and "schmoozy," a game where "charity begins at home" rather than "an eye for an eye" is the watchword. But that kind of mutually agreed upon "toleration" aside, the game as played with nine wickets and two stakes nevertheless has rules to follow.

I then explain the basics of American croquet, as played with six wickets and one stake and as endorsed by the USCA (whose rules for the nine-wicket croquet game generally played in our backyards are also adhered to here), and of British or international croquet, also played with six wickets and a single stake and sometimes referred to as English or "Association" croquet (after the British Croquet Association).

In order not to swamp the reader with too much information at once, I have made an effort to "walk through" each type of game a bit, following the course of the ball, leaving discussion of types of shots (as distinguished from strokes) and particular strategies—important to *all* croquet games—to a separate chapter. Without question, all three games can be played with great fun and, usually, with fervor, for as Thoreau noted, "The savage in man is never quite eradicated." Playing far into the night still is a likely outcome of all three games once the appetite grows; in any version of the game one might well say with Walt Whitman, "My voice goes after what my eyes cannot reach" as the ball goes off into the darkness and one howls with delight or outrage depending on whose ball it is. Agony and ecstasy.

Basic Backyard Croquet (Nine Wickets)

Many Americans play croquet in their own yards or the yards of friends. In so doing they are part of the essential tradition of the game, for it has always been played in that kind of setting. Granted, many of the large expansive lawns and "greenswards" of nineteenth-century England as well as the perfectly manicured lawns along the eastern coast of the United States (which by the end of the nineteenth century were decoratively peopled with croquet players) were bigger and better lawns than those typical today, yet they still *were* lawns.

Most people begin playing croquet with friends and family in simple yard settings on lawns that are anything but perfect. You may have hit a wicket that lay flat in the grass with a lawnmower, as you stayed up too late to remember counting the wickets as you pulled them up, and probably there is a redesigned coat hanger in the set because one wicket was thrown out accidentally. But basic backyard croquet, as it has come to be known, *is* croquet, and knowing how to play it correctly is important.

First, one must set up the croquet court: lay out the wickets and stakes. Here there is a fair amount of license, depending not only on the size, shape, and terrain of the lawn space you have available but also on the intended level of formality. In the most ideal conditions, the court should be laid out as illustrated in figure 1, on a flat plot of ground 100 feet long and 50 feet wide. If the court is to be smaller, either through desire (some people are "into small"—as with *nouvelle cuisine*) or because of space limitations, simply keep the same proportions of two-to-one in length and width and adjust the wicket placements accordingly.

The first wicket to be placed is the one located in the exact center of the rectangle. It should be equidistant from both sides and from both ends. Then it is simply a matter of making the two "ends" of the layout symmetrical. You then "line up" on that central wicket and walk six feet in from one end (and the ends are generally referred to as north and south, the sides east and west, though I find it sometimes is helpful simply to think in terms of left and right and up and down, so I take some license) and place a stake, and then walk six feet in from the other end and place a stake. Now you have formed a straight line. You add to it by placing two wickets in front of each stake at six-foot intervals. Now you have lengthened your straight

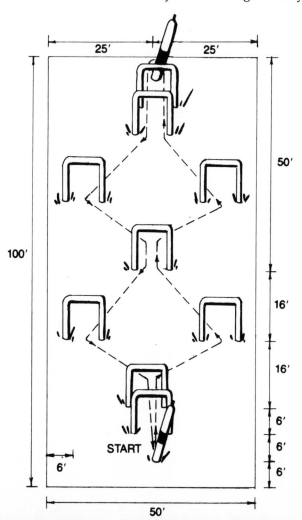

Figure 1. The basic course of the ball and placement of the wickets and stakes in American nine-wicket croquet.
Drawing by Suzanne T. Reaske.

line into one consisting of five wickets with a stake at each end. If this is beginning to give you a Druid-like feeling of re-creating Stonehenge, don't despair: It gets easier (and who knows, maybe the gods used the large wicketlike structures for their own game). As a child I used to enjoy bending down and looking straight down the lawn from behind one stake all the way to the other. The "tunnel" formed had a kind of mystery that has not yet completely left me.

Stakes, incidentally, were used by surveyors for many years to mark out land and lots. The idea of "staking out" such lines evolved into the concept of staking off things as a kind of protection; then people began to "stake" ponies and horses in place, people in place for punishment, and so forth (earlier Nero, of course, had staked and burned people). "Stakes" have to do with wagered amounts, loans, and have acquired other seemingly endless connotations. When you stake out a course, you are part of a long and interesting etymological heritage. Well, fairly interesting anyway.

If you have been counting (and I realize that nine wickets and two stakes carry you past your ten fingers), you now have four wickets left. Two should be placed on each side of the field, six feet in from the sides and fourteen feet from the middle where the central wicket is (this is for those of you who really want to get out and, you know, *measure away*). Now you have set up the layout in accordance with the "approved" rules of the United States Croquet Association. You should feel as satisfied as when you straighten a picture on the wall, square off a pile on the corner of your desk, or get the throw rug edge parallel with the front of the sofa (the latter activity drove E. B. White crazy!).

It is easy (well, possible anyway) to adapt this layout to virtually any lawn. If you do not have sufficient space (talking only about the game, not your relationships), just remember that the principles are the same. You want to come as close as you can to making a rectangle twice as long as it is wide. Then measure in from the ends and the sides to find the center. Then set up the same "symmetry" as illustrated, not worrying about the specific dimensions but maintaining the *same proportions*.

Fine, you say, but I end up with a wicket in a ditch, one in the middle of a garden, and I have to place a stake against a tree! At this point you need to be as cavalier as possible, take a deep breath, and remind yourself that this is a *game*. On the occasions when I feel compelled to read books or manuals on croquet, I sometimes feel as if I am studying to take college SAT exams. Or worse yet, the GRE or the LSAT. *Ergo,* simply move the wicket near to the gully or leave it there (in miniature golf, after all, the course is purposely filled with such hilarities in the form of obstacles). The same approach applies to the stake by the tree. Move the stake a little. Or if that makes you uncomfortable, let the tree *be* the stake. It's wood, after all. That's the kind of assertion a more formal croquet player will pounce on, but so be it! Like Walt Whitman, I utter the words democratic, the words *en masse.*

The main thing to keep in mind is that when you are playing croquet in your backyard or in a friend's yard (the latter necessarily having a definitional short-life as the rivalry accelerates), it is not a matter of life and death. And as for the state of your croquet court, you might want to bear in mind Frank Lloyd Wright's comment about simply making a house fit into the landscape: "No house should ever be *on* any hill or on anything. It should be *of* the hill, belonging to it, so hill and house could live together each the happier for the other." Let your court be *of* your yard.

Once the layout for your game is complete (remember, Stonehenge was harder), players select mallets and balls. This is fairly easy! The colors on the stake are a guide to which player goes first, which second, and so forth—the order of play is blue, red, black, and yellow. If you are playing against one player (see chapter 6), one person plays both the blue and black (I find it easier to say "black and blue" to myself, then change the order; that way I at least get the colors together without feeling like an idiot by going over and really, you know, *studying* the stake), and the opponent plays the red and yellow. If you are playing partners, the same division is made. The point is for opponents, whether two or four, to alternate.

The game usually begins with a toss of the coin, with one team or player choosing to go either first and third or second and fourth. If there is no coin (Fred never carries any money, on the court or at a restaurant . . . he's into his gold card), you can take shots from a single spot to see who can get closest to a stake or (my preference) simply "duke it out" with your fingers, as in childhood. The player with blue starts by placing the ball one mallet's length from the stake in front of the two wickets. You receive an extra stroke for going through each wicket. So the goal is to get through both of the wickets at once, thereby winning two strokes. Typically, you will go over to the right-hand side (east) with your first extra stroke and get through the first side wicket with your second extra stroke. (In some private clubs, where the play is more formal, only one extra stroke is earned for going through both of the stake wickets, but in general two is preferred.) The main incentive for trying to get through both wickets at once, even if you often end up missing the second wicket—which is a real pain because then you have to come back and try to get through it again—is to earn those two extra strokes. And before you have a chance you will, in all likelihood—especially if Fred's turn is coming up, and sending you is *all* he cares about—be hit by another ball and quite possibly be "sent" either away or out of position to go through the wicket anyway. Which is why some croquet games are lost in the first few moments of the game. And why, while it was nice of Steve and Wendy to invite you over, it was rotten of him to put you and your partner, Jill, out of commission so quickly.

Fortunately, backyard croquet provides—with its imperfect lawn and unpredictable bumps and lumps (and in our yard mole holes)—lots of opportunities for other players to run into trouble. Some players even *purposely* "booby trap" their lawn to increase the number of ways one can have problems. This is unquestionably a form of gallows humor. Such booby traps tend to have a "leveling" effect by minimizing the importance of skill and increasing the role of luck.

There is something wonderful about the feel of grass beneath bare feet—a freedom, a freshness, an at-one-with-nature effect—that must be weighed against the danger of placing a bare foot on the ball and then swinging a hard mallet at it. Of course you only place your foot on your ball to "send" the other, now-adjacent ball to some other location. It is, of course, strategically very helpful to send an oppo-

O

nent's ball to an awkward location. The ball is temporarily in a real fix and unable to hinder *you* as you progress to the next wicket. My older sister always had a way of curling her toes right around the ball like a sloth, and as a child she was always able to whack away without injury, or so it seemed (she did everything so well, and so competitively, that to this day I carry in my wallet a score sheet of the one time I managed somehow to beat her in the word game called Boggle).

You can, of course, go through life with a battered big toe, as it is usually the opposite foot from the direction you are swinging the mallet that gets used. If you have had a few drinks, which for some in backyard croquet is almost *de rigueur,* your toes can become even more violable . . . but the grass feels so good. It's not a decision to be made lightly. Of course, over the years you may have been piqued to observe Steve's progression in croquet away from martinis to gin and tonic to white wine to white wine *spritzers* (real watery at that)— it has been so obvious that he has come to value skill and victory (yes, superiority) more than a good time and friendship.

For the player who goes first—let's say it's you—your only consideration is to get through the first two wickets and, if possible, over to the right and through the next one. If you can make your first shot over to the right and make your ball stop just past the wicket but still in front of it, you can then try to hit it hard through the wicket toward the center wicket. As you have earned another stroke for passing through your third wicket, you can, in the best of circumstances, get through your fourth (center) wicket.

Let's take up the second player, Steve, assuming a game of four people playing partners. Steve started playing croquet when he was a young boy. It was fun back then and a natural part of those halcyon summer days. Now grown-up, Steve plays croquet more intensely than before. He's a good guy, and your friend, but you really will die if he wins. And he knows it.

Steve sets the ball in place and proceeds just as you did. However, there is a difference. Steve plays in a universe where there are now two "alive" balls. If Steve hits your ball, he acquires two additional strokes, a "croquet stroke" and a "continuation stroke." So Steve may, for example, decide to hit his ball hard through both of the first two wickets up to the middle of the court and then, having earned two strokes, use those to hit your ball. He may then decide to move your ball far away from where his partner's ball will be, or at least make it hard for you to continue very successfully at all. This is probably how Steve would do it.

Having hit your ball and "done something with it" (there is, in croquet, a whole continuous questioning of "What are you going to do with/to me?" that expresses the fearfulness the game eventually instills in all players), Steve then returns to line up on the third wicket. There are a lot of things that could be happening by this point, but let's keep it simple and typical.

The third player, your partner, Jill, enters the game in a way different from either of the first two players because she enters a universe where there are now already two alive balls in play, one of which is hung up down the field somewhere (yours) and Steve's, which is over by the wicket on the right side.

Using two additional strokes gained from going through the first two wickets, Jill can either go down the field to help you (by using one stroke to come down to you and the next to hit you, thereby again earning two additional strokes that can be used to bring you back to the beginning of the course), or temporarily forget you and instead proceed to the area of the first wicket on the right. Using two strokes, there is a pretty good chance that she will be able to go over there, hit Steve's ball, get through the wicket, then hit Steve's ball again, and send it into a difficult spot while advancing on the way. Of course everything hinges on Jill's being able to hit Steve's ball. The dread of croquet—the part that sends you into craziness and hostile fits—is not simply missing the ball you want to hit but *just* missing it, or stopping very close to it. For one thing is certain—that ball will show little mercy as it turns on you and does to you what you had planned to do to it. Mark Twain once observed that if a man could feed either a dog or a friend, it would be wiser to feed the dog because the dog would never turn on him. This is particularly true when playing against a guy like Steve.

Now, let's think about all of this a little longer. The object of the game is to get you and your partner, Jill, through all the wickets in the right order, which means (see the illustration on page 43) going through—read this as if at a square dance, please—the first wicket on the right, then through the center wicket, then the second on the right, then through the two at the end, hitting the stake, coming back through those two, out to your right (coming back in the opposite direction), and (no do-si-do) repeating the same progression to return. To get your two balls through this course before the other team gets theirs through is what counts, so every time either you or your partner take a turn, you need to decide what to do.

This is where the game becomes kind of dicey. Jill confers with you. You suggest that she forget about trying to help you (maybe you are hoping she will be even nicer to you later—after the game; this is also called paybacks in the language of love if not croquet) and just advance herself. So she does. Here you might actually show a touch of surprise. You *did* tell her to abandon you, but couldn't she have resisted? In any case, Jill proceeds as planned, but then she screws up by missing Steve's ball. Her turn is over.

Jill may now begin to blame you for advising her to try to hit Steve's ball. "I was too far away and you know I'm not that good a shot anyway." Why didn't you tell her to come down by you? The argument may wear thin, but Steve and Wendy are looking at each other with wonderful self-satisfaction. It is in their best interest to see not only your partnership in this game but indeed your whole relationship come apart (such as it is; they don't really know, but the better they think it is, the greater their satisfaction in destroying it). What moves they now make will, in part, reflect personality.

Now enter the fourth ball. Here comes Wendy to help Steve. You chose to go first and third when you won the initial flip of the coin and then the other colors followed in order. Up until now Wendy has been watching from the sidelines, eagerly getting ready to enter the game. Wendy likes a good game of croquet. She is always calling up friends and saying "Come over for a fun game of croquet." It isn't always good, and it isn't always fun. But she and Steve are in this thing together. Why go to Europe when they can have friends over

O

for croquet? Wendy knows that when she enters the fray, there will be an incredible number of possibilities. Of course she still has to begin like the first three players and pass through the first two wickets. She can advance herself, help Steve, wreak havoc on you and Jill, and maybe accomplish all three. Here personality dynamics come heavily into play.

Sometimes the fourth player decides to go around and hit everybody. For one thing—and aside from the wonderful *clack* of ball hitting ball—this lets player number four receive an incredible amount of attention and feel a little like Clint Eastwood at the same time (more than one croquet player has been heard to mutter, "Go ahead—make my day"). He can play and play and play, hit balls, go through wickets, hit some more, maybe even play the entire course—sort of like shooting the moon in a card game of hearts. It is strictly center-stage business.

Alternatively, the fourth player can try to avoid falling into the problems he has seen befall everyone else in the game by outsmarting them all, by concentrating on playing as if they didn't even exist. Or he can throw himself fully into the agenda of helping his partner. This St. Bernard kind-of-stuff can go a long way to help, at least temporarily, a deteriorating relationship. It can also reinforce unfortunate notions or preconceptions of wimpishness.

When a player hits another player, he is then "dead" on that ball until he goes through a wicket. (Being "dead" on a ball means you cannot hit that ball again until you have passed through a wicket—at which point you are "live" on that same ball once again.) Each player can, however, hit *all* three of the other balls without passing through a wicket—finally becoming dead on all three—but then after he goes through the wicket he is live on them all again. The worst position to be in is to be dead on two or three balls, however, and kept from going through a wicket. This is where the emasculation side of the game can become truly outrageous, as one player is kept—and the language is almost unutterable—either "two-ball dead" or (worse yet, can it be true?) "three-ball dead" for much of the game because he is unable to get through a wicket and become "live" again.

There is little that is more wimpy than having to endure this kind of low-life existence.

As the game progresses, all players continue to try to advance through the wickets while simultaneously trying to prevent the opposition from doing so. Of course, certain things happen. For one thing, a ball can go out of bounds. If you set your boundaries with a string (which is not a typical procedure for most), the ball is considered out of bounds if it is more than 50 percent across the string. When this happens, it gets brought back in by a mallet head's length. If a ball gets "wicketed," meaning that it stops without being all the way through the wicket, it does not count as being through unless when you run the long side of your mallet head down the side of the wicket you entered, it does not touch the ball.

○

When you succeed in having your ball hit another ball, and assuming you are "live" on that ball—and certainly not in that dreadful state of being "two-ball dead" or (gasp, pain) "three-ball dead"—you can then choose from a large variety of *shots* (see discussion in chapter 5), including placing your foot on your own ball (called "footing the ball," one of the more obvious and pleasantly stupid instances of literal language in the game) and hitting it to make the other ball travel while yours stays where it is, and so forth. Which shots to use will depend on your particular objectives at certain points, and it is by learning *which* shots to use *when* that you will advance in your skill as a player. But right now we simply want to focus on the progress of the game.

You and Jill are now locked into a state of war with Steve and Wendy. Wendy's warm invitation to "come by for a fun game of croquet" has been transformed into a pull-no-punches battle. That Wendy can try not just to hit Jill, but to separate her and you as if she were pulling apart mating crabs has shown her for the real antagonist she is.

Wendy decides to hit you, thereby earning two additional strokes. She elects to send your ball to a remote spot of the court, then uses her remaining shot to clear a wicket. She then positions herself for the next wicket with a good long shot. She has placed you virtually out of reach of anyone, which of course means that it is unlikely you will be able to hit another ball on your turn. The best you can do is either to take a long-shot try at hitting a distant ball (you might be surprised at how you can succeed at this!) or, simply do your best to get closer to the wicket you need to clear next. One thing is certain: When you get the chance, you will try very hard to send Wendy's ball in the same way. Any illusions you may have had that her "nice" side might prevail have now been fully dispelled.

Eventually one player goes through all of the wickets and back again. At that point he has what is known as a "rover" ball. He then must make a decision. He can hit the stake (or peg) and in so doing end his participation in the game ("peg out"). His ball is simply removed from the lawn and the game. More often, though, this rover ball is used to assist the partner to advance so that the two of them can end the game together; because it is only when both balls on a team have gone through all of the wickets and *both* pegged out that the game has been won. (The same is true if two people are playing, with each player controlling two balls.)

The rover ball is out of the game when it hits the final peg. However, in the meantime it can continue to *rove* (hence the name) around the course, hitting other balls and winning two shots, just as before; and as the rover has already passed through all the wickets, it can no longer earn extra strokes for going through wickets again. The rover ball, which takes its turn in regular order, represents an irritatingly free and relatively easier mode of existence to the opponent players and a godsend to the rover's partner. The rover maneuvers to aid his partner and impede the progress of the opposition.

It is a wonderful feeling to be a rover. Even having the name "rover" attached to your ball makes you feel free, possibly even superior. Especially if Steve is still in his more earthly, prerover state. It is like being able to do anything you want—but only up to a point, as eventually someone else will become a rover and you may still be prevented from winning. Here you need to think hard about the line between helping your partner and wreaking havoc on everyone else. Also, it should be noted that at some point you must either hit the stake yourself or have your partner hit you into the stake in order to be out and finished.

There is yet another complication to finishing the game. If your *opponent* makes your ball hit the stake, you then must pick up the ball and stay out for the two next turns. On your third turn you must place your ball a mallet head's length from the stake and go hit the stake at the opposite end of the field. After this you have regained life as a rover once again. Thus the freedom and happiness of being a rover, like other points of glory in the game, are always subject to reversal. Yogi Berra's famed pronouncement "The game ain't over till it's over" might well be remembered if anyone gets too self-congratulatory (see, for example, " 'The game is done! I've won, I've won!' / Quoth she, and whistles thrice" (Coleridge's *Rime of the Ancient Mariner*). In a "fun" version of backyard croquet, players can agree to play "poison" at the end. In this game, when a ball has passed through all the wickets, it becomes a deadly poisonous creature that kills on contact. A poison ball hits another ball and thereby garners the vicarious and much-popularized satisfaction of exterminating that ball. It is like this "gentle" game to have a very satisfying finale that allows for total death and instant destruction of one's enemies!

In any case, it is the pattern of advance and decline, of progress and retrograde motion, that becomes the essential dialectic of the game, that gives it a rhythm. Like the proverbial wheel of fortune, the croquet player gets lifted up only to be sunk down, hopefully to be lifted up once again—perhaps by one's partner. There is always hope, until, of course, either you or your partner (or both) fall what seems an impossible distance behind, at which point friendships get tested and revenge instincts begin to deepen. Uncontrollably, you begin to distance yourself from the game at hand and fix your eye on the next match.

Two further notes about the finale of the game: First, if you are a rover ball and you hit another ball and then your ball goes on to hit the stake, this is not considered staking out or pegging out. The minute your ball has hit the other ball, you have short-circuited the

○

process, as it were, and you are entitled to take two additional strokes as you would after any roquet (which is a term used anytime your ball hits another ball).

If you choose to, you can peg out with one of these strokes. Whether or not to peg out depends on a decision, arrived at carefully through an off-to-the-sides tryst with your partner (under ideal circumstances, and if the opponents will give you the time alone—sometimes opponents take on the same omnipresence as mothers-in-law because they *know* if they leave you alone you may well figure things out, especially how to work around them). Do you want to let one of you escape completely from the maddening crowd of the game? What, after all, is the value of being self-"sidelined"? If you stay in and try to "help" your partner, you may in fact jeopardize winning. It's a tough choice. Which is why you need to give it some careful thought. After all, you have worked hard (well, fairly hard) to get through all the wickets. Pegging out is the natural final step. But do you take it? People are now believed to die not of "old age" but of various "diseases." You can, by adopting a plan of exercise (which rules out croquet), prolong your life. Is it worth it? What is the reason? You can have the same kind of existentially framed discussion about pegging out. As with Hamlet, readiness is all.

Second, in case it needs saying one more time, the game ends *only* when both balls on one team have completed all wickets and hit the stake. This is why you may have to turn the car lights on as it gets dark and you continue to relish knocking one another around.

Let's think back on this basic game just a little bit more. I promise "a little." The principles are clear: Advance through all of the wickets in order, help your partner to do the same, and both hit the final stake for your victory. Along the way try not to go out of bounds but to leave yourself sitting right near the edge of the boundary from time to time where it may prove harder to hit you (see "tice" in the glossary). Or hit your ball into a corner (known—really—as "cornering the ball"). Go through wickets and, at times, try to hide behind them a bit so that you cannot be hit. There are probably no other things to hide behind besides wickets, other balls, and maybe an occasional rock or tuft of weeds, depending on the state of your croquet lawn, although more than one player has tried to *stand* in such a way as to protect or hide his ball (or to point to an airplane or bird to distract the opponent's attention). Above all, remember Benjamin Franklin's wisdom when he said that "the cat in gloves catches no mice"—be aggressive. Of course it was also Franklin who advised, "Keep your eyes wide open *before* marriage, half shut *afterward*." Don't expect your croquet partner to be perfect! But *do* find ways to make it clear to your opponent that his or her partner carries a considerable set of shortcomings.

○

The basic nine-wicket game of croquet becomes "user friendly" in that people do not have to get *too* official or use language that seems too unfamiliar to enjoy playing the game informally with friends (just look at "corner" and "footing," for example). And if you want to, make things easier on one another, by letting someone (Wendy, maybe) take all the shots needed in the beginning in order to pass through at least the first two wickets, or take the shot again if she moves the ball just a tiny bit when more was hoped for. Life will not come to an end over such acts of kindness.

On the other hand, basic backyard croquet has everything needed to bring out the beast in you. Let it happen. There is a certain amount of fun in going through so *many* wickets (they all look alike but you are meeting them in different places), and in having the chance to hit not one but two stakes, as the thud of hitting the stake has a wonderful sensation about it.

Now that the United States Croquet Association has recognized nine-wicket croquet and outlined the rules, regulations, ideal court size, and so forth, perhaps the game will continue to win back the respect it deserves.

American Croquet (Six Wickets)

The preferred game of many croquet enthusiasts and of the growing number of competitive croquet players (some would say that's redundant) is the "official" American version of croquet. As with En-

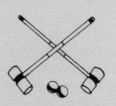

GEORGE WASHINGTON JOHNSON
NAMED PRESIDENT

The first formal organization of croquet in the United States took place on February 12, 1880, when the National Croquet League was created in Philadelphia. Interestingly enough, the first president had a highly appropriate name: George Washington Johnson, of the Lemon Hill Croquet Club. The event brought together representatives from eighteen clubs, and their first order of business—wouldn't you *guess?*—was to make the wickets somewhat smaller and the balls somewhat bigger. This wasn't the first time that the game had been narrowed a bit. Perhaps at some future point we will be pushing marbles through inverted half paperclips—at least in the literary tradition of ancient Greece when suitors of Penelope supposedly fought for her by playing a good game of marbles.

glish croquet, there are six wickets and one stake. The game is the one played in American club competitions and by colleges and universities that field croquet teams. (Colleges in the New England Collegiate Croquet Association include Brown, Cornell, Harvard, Pine Manor, the Rhode Island School of Design, the University of Massachusetts, Wellesley, Williams, and Yale.)

Six-wicket croquet is extremely appealing because it alternates long distances between wickets with shorter distances between wickets and because it is designed to move you around the field in a very interesting sequence. There are endless opportunities to "reach out and touch someone." The popularity and status of American six-wicket croquet as it is now played will, in all likelihood, continue for the indefinite future.

First, let us consider the official layout for the game and then, once again, walk through a typical progression on the field, mindful as before that the nature of specific shots and the strategies for using them are presented in chapter 5.

American (six-wicket) croquet is played on a more squared-off rectangle than that of nine-wicket croquet. The "official" recommended dimensions are 105 feet in length and 84 feet in width, but nontournament courts can be set up on a smaller scale, so long as the same five-to-four ratio of length to width is maintained. Obviously it is helpful to have a large, open rectangular area of backyard in which to set up such a course. The six wickets are once again positioned in an entirely symmetrical fashion, and as before, it is easiest to measure from the ends and the sides to find the exact center of the court where the single stake should be placed (see figure 2) as the first step in setting up.

As before, you line up the wickets to form a straight line with this central stake by placing a single wicket 31½ feet in from each end. Then you are ready to place the four corner wickets, each of which is set 21 feet in from each side, again in perfect symmetry. If you are planning a court of different size, the important thing is to keep the distances proportionally the same and place the wickets in the same symmetry. For example, always center the court with the central stake, line up the two opposite end wickets, and walk the four corner wickets in from each corner. There is a north and south and east and west for your guidance, but I will talk in terms of left and right as before, because I think that's easier. My father-in-law is the only one I know who not only says the wind is from the northeast but that he is walking southwest; my inability to do the same has always been a disappointment to him.

American (six-wicket) croquet opens very differently from the nine-wicket game. The order of play is the same as before, and is indicated on the stake: blue, red, black, and yellow. A coin is flipped

O

○

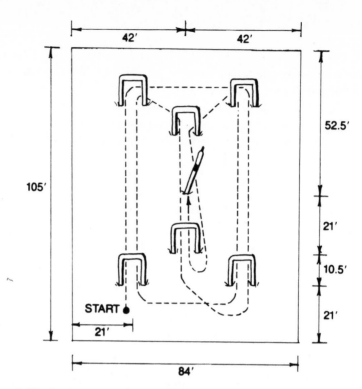

Figure 2. The basic course of the ball and placement of the wickets and center stake in American six-wicket croquet. *Drawing by Suzanne T. Reaske.*

and the winner can choose either to go first and third, with blue and black (pop quiz: Do you remember *how* to remember the pairing of balls on each team?), or second and fourth, with red and yellow. Let's walk through some of a typical game so that the rules can emerge from the process of thinking about how you and the others will proceed.

The first player (and each successive player) begins by placing his ball a mallet's length in front of the first wicket, positioned in the lower left-hand corner of the field. Here we need to think differently than before about being "dead" or alive on other balls. Your ball is dead when you begin this game and stays dead until you have passed through the first wicket, at which point you become alive and you also earn an extra shot. *But,* in this game if you do not get through the first wicket and thus are dead, you can hit any other ball that is also dead. You can send it or do what you want. If you send your partner's ball through a wicket, you make that ball alive, although it doesn't earn the extra stroke you earn when you put your own ball through the wicket. Got it? Believe me, this is easy compared to what some books tell you!

There is more to understand about the opening of six-wicket croquet. Once you are through the wicket, you are dead on all balls that have *not* gone through the wicket. If you go through the first wicket and hit a ball that is dead, you just get one additional stroke for going through the wicket and the other ball is replaced to where it was sitting before you hit it. Once you are through the first wicket, you proceed to try to hit only those balls on which you are alive. In these instances, as in nine-wicket croquet, you earn two additional strokes. Most people playing the six-wicket game don't "waste" a stroke to "send" another ball because they are determined to clear the next wicket, which is easier to do with two strokes. In fact, it is often best to proceed in that way, and *then* go back to hit the ball again, hopefully in an "injurious" way, and still have two new strokes to go on to clear the *next* wicket.

Back to the beginning. Let's assume that Wendy goes first (a year has passed and you're willing to give her a try again) and misses the wicket. You are standing off to the side. Smiling. Steve, having announced that he's now running daily and eating a *lot* of bran, is still showing that familiar discomfort through the red "rushes" on the sides of his neck. Good. The second player, Jill (you're still together but this weekend is planned as the one when you try to decide "once and for all" whether your relationship has a future—bad environment for that, but oh, well), decides to hit Wendy's ball (good again) and therefore earns two additional strokes. She uses one to further inconvenience Wendy (God, this is getting even better) while, with the same shot, better positioning herself (see "shots" in chapter 5) to get through the first wicket. She still has another stroke left and cannot hit Wendy again so she makes a long shot to get herself down to the far upper corner on the same side of the court. This is one of the major underlying enjoyments of this variety of croquet—if it is satisfying to position your ball in front of the right wicket at a relatively short distance away, well then, traveling all the way down the course to land in precisely the right spot for the second wicket is even better. The long distance between the side wickets, which as we will see gets traveled twice in opposite directions, allows for the development of considerable skill.

Because you are going to play clockwise and counterclockwise through the same sideline alley wickets, clips are used (only in formal play, and probably not in this "fun" game) to indicate which direction you are traveling. Clips are placed on top of the wickets when you are going (north) and on the side of the wickets when you are returning (south). As the game (and the evening) progresses, you may not remember which way a particular ball besides your own is intending to go through a wicket.

Now Steve enters. He has lost weight since last summer. Has he become lean and mean? Or weak and meek? Wait and see. He has a choice to make because there are already two balls at work in the field. He could hit Wendy's ball and try to manipulate the two of them through the first wicket, as they are both still dead and can be used in that way. This will bring them both to life. Then Steve can use Wendy either to take two shots to get down to the far end and hit the opponent's ball or to get both himself and Wendy down the field (and again, the type of shots used will be tied up with the strategy, as explained later). Steve opts for the latter, and it works.

Now it is your turn—at last. You find yourself alone at this south end of the field and you may want to try to make a very hard drive through the first wicket, in order to get up by everyone else and begin using all three of the balls now assembled there to advance both you and Jill (at this early point in the weekend, you suspect that you're both leaning toward hoping that you'll stay together). The danger, as always, is in not getting through the first wicket by hitting the ball too hard. You may thereby isolate yourself from the other three balls for a considerable amount of time, and possibly for the whole game. If you miss the wicket, it may leave you feeling as if you have been consigned to a leper colony, for no one is going to go anywhere near you until your partner is able to help, which, given the length of the course, may not be for a long time. And you're not quite sure *where* Jill is anyway. She may be planning to go it alone. Despite your good vibes, she's used the words "freedom" and "autonomy" six or seven times in the last day.

The psychology of this situation is itself worth commenting on. Your partner in croquet quite often has to decide whether to help you now or operate aggressively in an independent way, trying to travel the whole course as quickly as possible and then and only then going back and helping *you* get through the course. What's going on between you and your partner personally, now and in both the collective past and the fantasized future, has a great deal of bearing on the decisions you make. Don't let anyone tell you otherwise. Often, in fact, certain people who are tuned in to the full personality of someone else will really play on their pity at *any* point in the game. If he is about to be treated badly or ignored, he may say, for example, "Oh, no, why am I *always* picked on, do you hate me because I wouldn't _____? Is that it? There has to be a reason you're doing this." Even a tough opponent can be weakened in this way. If not, try crying.

Let's assume that you do get through and join the others. All players have taken their first turns, certain patterns are established, and the battle is now fully joined. You all proceed to travel, as you are able to, and *ideally by making "breaks"* (discussed in the next chapter) across to the far corner, located diagonally opposite from where you began, then all the way down the other long (east) side, at which point you then proceed to go up the middle of the course through the two center line wickets, *bypassing the stake as you go,* then over to the far left corner and back down, across the bottom, back up the side, then into the center (this time you may want to all join hands and allemande left) . . . carry on . . . to the stake at last, then relax and quote Shakespeare:

Fear no more the heat o' the sun,
Nor the furious winter's rages;
Thou thy worldly task hast done,
Home art gone, and ta'en thy wages.
Golden lads and girls all must,
As chimney-sweepers, come to dust.

○

Right? No. Remember first that there is the rover stage to pass through—same as before. When a ball has passed progressively through all of the "twelve" wickets (6 wickets × 2 directions), it becomes a rover ball. If it hits the stake or is hit into the stake *by another rover ball*, it has then completed the game. You win the game if your two balls hit the stake before both of the opposing team's balls hit it. Your partner cannot hit you into the stake if he has not yet achieved the same rover-ball status. This can be a problem, as can other configurations. As before, the rover ball can hit the other balls once, each in a turn, and gain new life on them only by going through any wicket in *any* direction.

Many of the same rules apply to both six-wicket and nine-wicket croquet. To be all the way through a wicket, you must be able to run a mallet down the entering side so the ball does not move (no fair bending a wicket, though you wouldn't be the first). If your ball goes out of bounds, you place it back in by a mallet head's length. You do not receive any gain for going through a "wrong" wicket (that is, not the next wicket in correct sequence). When using clips—remember, a year has passed, maybe you're into clips, or maybe Steve is; it would be like him, wouldn't it?—to indicate your next required wickets, you once again place the clip on the side of the next wicket you are aiming for when you begin in one direction (the first six wickets, in effect), and then place the clip on top of the wicket when going through the rest of them. Most people in nontournament play do not bother using clips, but if you do, remember that the correct time to remove the clip from a wicket is immediately after you have gone through it; you then proceed to place it in the proper position on the next wicket you must go through.

Here is a particularly important rule. When you make a *roquet*, you then can pick up your ball (known unimaginatively at this moment as "ball-in-hand") and place it against the other ball, just as before. You can either hit both or hold your foot (recall my earlier exposition of the phrase, "footing the ball") on your ball while you send the other one. If you are hitting your ball and *not* footing it, it is essential that the other ball *move*. If it does not move at all, you receive a penalty: Your turn ends, and thus you forfeit the right to your second or continuing stroke. Of course, this situation depends on the eyesight of all in the group. Did the ball move? Who says it didn't? How can you prove it? Generally people are fairly reasonable about this, but the level of intensity with which this rule is observed varies. It is worth appealing to your finer instincts by recalling Grantland Rice's well-known lines in his *Alumnus Football* about how the One Great Scorer marks down not the fact that you won or lost, "but how you played the game."

You always get one stroke when it is your turn unless you earn an extra stroke by going through a wicket or by roqueting (hitting) a ball. Your own ball is then—remember?—known as the ball-in-hand, and you place the two balls in contact, as discussed. How you proceed depends on which type of shot you select, as explained in the next chapter. As you "use" the other balls to earn additional shots to advance through further wickets, you should remember that only Jill's ball is a friendly one (exceptions can be made, either to flirt or to confuse). For that reason, it is best to avoid being dead on your partner's ball for as much of the time as you can, mostly by roqueting your partner's ball when you feel there is a good chance to get through a wicket and be quickly alive on that ball again.

What happens if someone takes a turn at the wrong time, that is, out of order? This can happen particularly as the night wears on and darkness sets in. It can also happen when someone tries to cheat. Fred, for sure. And would you put it past Wendy? Usually someone will intervene just before the shot is taken, either by calling out (possibly in a profane way: "What the _____ are you doing? It's not your _____ turn!"), by tackling the player and hurling him to the ground, or by creating a distraction of some sort long enough to divert the player's attention from his ball. But if such measures fail, the player is penalized. The balls are replaced to where they were and the offending player misses his next turn.

Most important in all of this is that the mistake *must be noticed* by the opposition. If you play out of turn and no one notices it, or doesn't realize it until *after* you have played, nothing happens. There is, then, a small but attractive incentive in going out of turn, especially if you think no one will notice. Croquet is unusual in this regard, for while you are not encouraged to cheat, the rules cover how you may do so. In a fun-loving nontournament game it is worth trying to take undue advantage of your enemies once in a while. Unless you're playing for money, which is *très gauche.* To quote William Hazlitt, "We never do anything well till we cease to think about the manner of doing it." Possibly by just playing when we feel like it instead of when we're supposed to we may come up with a fantastic, fully artful, and overpowering—indeed convincing—shot. Others may be so impressed that they will forget whose turn it is (and it is not at all unusual in a "gentle but wicket" game for one person to play out of turn and thereby stimulate *everyone* to "get out of sync"). And if we go out of turn in good fun, not exactly to cheat, well, what of it? Only croquet will tolerate such business. In hockey you might get away with high-sticking without a penalty. In basketball you might get in an elbow. But playing ahead of your turn and getting away with it if no one notices is sort of like robbing a bank in broad daylight. Not to worry. Life's too short.

Just as going out of order is wrong, so is hitting a ball you are dead on and pretending you are alive on it. This is sort of like saying "I don't believe we've met" to someone you remember meeting very recently. The same rules prevail. If the opposition notices your error *before* they take their turn, you return the balls to where they were and you have, in effect, lost your turn. If it is not noted until after the opponent has played, then nothing happens. Sort of like cashing a bad check? But oh, well! You're out of there!

Because croquet is not a fast-paced "blood sport" but a slower more calculating one, akin to billiards and pool where the angles and relationships of the different balls are carefully studied before the shot is made, there are, in a curious way, almost more opportunities for unfair moves. Therefore, each player needs to be alert—defining alert in relative terms to mean *as alert* as everyone else. And of course croquet acquired its "tainted" immoral reputation at one point because it encouraged such deep-seated rivalry and aggression, not to mention its increasingly recognized and intimidating sexuality.

Here are a few things that might have happened in this hypothetical game in which Wendy went first, Jill second, Steve third, and you fourth. Let's assume that by the middle of the game you had all completed the first seven wickets—the teams are essentially even. This probably means that you and Jill and Steve and Wendy have both been trying to stay together as partners. Suddenly on his turn, Steve, being even more aggressive than you had remembered, decides to cut loose from the pack, go it alone, race the course with long daring shots. He takes off, leaving even Wendy confused by her sudden aloneness and vulnerability. "Why is he doing this to me?" she wonders. You and Jill should quickly suggest some unnerving reasons ("Maybe it's because you . . .").

You and Jill should then openly applaud Steve for his bravado in trying to rely on his skills independently as he sets out to distance himself. You should comment to one another that *down deep* Steve does not really care to play partners, that he has only been "using" Wendy. These comments should be uttered for Wendy's benefit, deepening her new and sudden insecurity. Make it unmanageable for her. Make her fearful (unless, of course, you have picked up on something new this summer and discovered that Wendy would be happy to see Steve go—"and take your compact discs with you!"). This should stimulate Wendy toward greater independence on her own part. Then they will have double trouble as they vie for power in their relationship.

Meanwhile, as you help stimulate the degeneration of the relationship between Steve and Wendy, you should try to act like the model couple you may in fact decide to become by the end of the

O

weekend. This may be the best test, after all, and things have been up in the air between you and Jill for much too long anyway. But don't get *too* chummy with Jill and inadvertently tip Steve and Wendy back into a bond that makes them feel they must kill you for your smugness and superiority. Just get on the *edge* of perfection as you and Jill relate. Don't go all the way. That could get pretty dicey!

As most people play croquet until one side wins (or, in a real party game, until someone passes out), very few amateur games make use of point scoring. Still, it should be noted that there is a "scoring" process for the game, a very simple one. Are you ready? You receive a point for each wicket you pass through. Thus, if you are playing six-wicket croquet, there is a total of twelve for one ball, plus a point for hitting the stake. This means that there are a total of twenty-six points available for either team, whether two players are competing and using two balls each or partners are playing. It is good to keep score if you believe you won't be able to finish the game, or if you simply want to determine at the outset that you will play, say, for one hour, and whichever team has the most points will win. Informally, it is possible simply to agree to play a "half game" of six or seven points and agree ahead how it will "end." You might, in fact, want to commit yourself to something less than a whole game just because you'd like a simple score-keeping experience—a good contrast to those complicated scoring word games that may have hurt you and your partner's relationship over the past winter.

While I have combined the discussion of strategy with the explanation of different shots, I should nevertheless note here that your goal is always to get you and your partner through as many wickets as quickly as possible and, in any event, ahead of the opposition. As with chess, you need to think ahead, to consider what is likely to happen on the opposition's part if you make such and such a move. There is a fair amount of probability involved in croquet, and the odds are that, faced with several alternatives, one intelligent, experienced player will make the same choice as another. (Except that pain-in-the-ass Fred. He can be rather fatuous in liking to go out of his way to be unpredictable.)

In this game, as in the nine-wicket game, you and Jill will attempt to stay together, to support and use one another, to advance through the wickets. Your hope is to capitalize—both literally and psychologically—on Steve's somewhat "spontaneous" solo departure. By focusing on making breaks while looking for subtle ways to make Wendy feel humiliated, you and Jill should be able to win this "fun game of croquet" that was Wendy's idea. In the end, you may even find you have, by sticking together, beaten Steve and Wendy quite badly. They *will*, of course, get over it—they *may* get even in the next game, assuming they're still speaking to each other—so don't apologize.

O

Association, or British Croquet (Also Six Wickets)

Although the official British croquet game (known also as "Association croquet" after the British Croquet Association) varies in only a relatively small number of ways from the American six-wicket game, the differences are such that the resulting games differ greatly in terms of strategy and pacing. It is, in general, a longer game, but certainly not without its own form of intensity and challenge. Of course, there will always be those on both sides of the Atlantic who turn up their mallets at the game as played across the sea, but I believe there are different kinds of fun to be had in both versions. It is sort of like trout fishing with flies or with worms—both are fun, so long as you catch a fish (although I suppose there might be a more appetizing analogy).

What *are* the main differences between British or Association croquet and American six-wicket croquet? The best way to learn them is to play a game. After a few preliminary comments, I'll get you together with Harriet and Charles, from England (no less).

First, let's consider the layout (see figure 3). Essentially the English and American versions are identical. The six wickets and stakes are placed in the same places on a court that is, properly, of the same size or, informally, at least of the same dimensions proportionally. However, in the English version they have some supposed "lines" inside the overall rectangle. First, there is what is known as the invisible "yard line," meaning that all the way around the inside of the

○

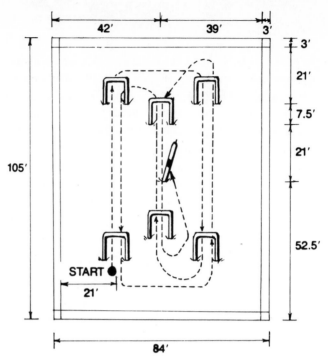

Figure 3. The basic course of the ball and placement of the wickets and center stake in British or Association six-wicket croquet. (Note the need to pass by and then return to the stake at the end, a key difference from American six-wicket croquet.) *Drawing by Suzanne T. Reaske.*

perimeter of the rectangle, at a distance of one yard from the edge, there is a line that creates a one-yard-deep zone area of space; when a ball is removed from the court (for example, knocked out of bounds either by oneself or the opponent), it is then placed inside this area *anywhere* (in the American version, you will recall that a ball being placed back in the game can be placed in only one mallet head's length). Second, there are two "baulk" lines in opposite corners. In the lower left-hand corner (south), a baulk line runs halfway across the field, and in the opposite corner (north and east), a baulk line runs halfway in to the center. These baulk areas constitute minicourts and are used to place the ball (again, *anywhere* in the area) to begin the game. Here we can see the similarity to the basic game of billiards;

in that game you place the cue ball behind a baulk line across one end in making opening shots (in more advanced billiards a series of four lines parallel to the cushions divide the table into nine compartments). In pool, if the opponent accidentally sinks the cue ball in a pocket, you then begin your turn by placing the cue ball wherever you want behind the baulk line (indicated by an imagined line through the "dot" on one end of the table). In British croquet it works the same way; it may be to your partner's advantage to knock him out of bounds and thereby provide him with an opportunity to reenter at a more strategic spot. A "baulk," incidentally, in the basic sense denotes simply a ridge of land that has not been plowed, thus forming a kind of natural divider. The baulk "lines" are basically important in conception, not in actuality. You do not literally create these lines on the court (or set up strings). Of course you might *want* to, which would be all right, I suppose.

O

What about the course of the ball? In British croquet you proceed through the wickets exactly as before, *except for the very last one.* As you come through the final wicket in British croquet, you have the stake behind you, pass through, and then *return* to hit the stake at the end (whereas in American croquet you come up and around, and pass through the wicket aiming yourself right at the stake). Otherwise the wickets are all played the same way as in American six-wicket croquet. If you are accustomed to playing American croquet, and especially if you mostly play nine-wicket croquet, this difference requires a little restraint. You may be tempted, if you have overshot, to want to come through the wicket and hit the stake at the same time. Americans always seem to want to accomplish two things at once. It is part of our "value-added" orientation (evident in two-for-one marketing lures). If you have Oscar Wilde in mind—"I can resist everything except temptation"—do not fear. Someone, certainly that pain-in-the-ass Fred if he is around, will probably yell coarsely at you ("What the _____ are you doing?") before you do it the wrong way. As the stake stands with a kind of phallic presence in the exact center of the course, radiating a Dionysian power, it is unlikely that the group will let you have a go at it until you have earned the right!

Aside from the play of the last wicket and the stake and the imaginary baulk lines, what else is different about British croquet?

Chief among the relatively few differences is that in British croquet you are "alive" on all balls *as soon as you start your next turn*. This is a *big* difference. Seriously. You can, for example, try to stretch and hit an opponent's ball in certain situations and sequences rather than worrying that you may become two-ball dead, three-ball dead, and so forth. Just as soon as your turn comes around again, you are completely reborn. Every time. This rule, established by the British Association in 1909, might make it appear that the English do not wish to keep anyone in a terrible fix for too long. To accept this interpretation too quickly would be a mistake, for the British game is every bit as aggressive as the American. The essential impact of this rule is that *there is less incentive to get yourself through all the wickets and more incentive to bring your partner along*. Because you do not have to clear a wicket to regain "life," you can instead help your partner and make progress together. This tends to make the English game a much longer one. And it is potentially more romantic. Still, in terms of numbers on a world-wide basis, it is not nearly as popular as American croquet, either among tournament players or beginners.

Another difference in British croquet is that as each team plays its two balls (still red and yellow and blue and black), in either a two-person game with each player playing two balls or a four-person game with two sets of partners playing two balls, you *do not have to alternate balls*. Instead of playing in a fixed color progression, the team that is red and yellow decides when it is its turn which of the two balls to play. You might play a blue ball three turns in a row, then your black one once or twice, and so forth. This solidifies the sense of partnership and leads to a different mood and a different set of strategies.

In American croquet when you hit an opponent's ball and knock it out of bounds, your turn simply ends and the opponent's ball is placed back on the court by a mallet head's length (as is your ball if it is out too). You are still "live" on that ball.

In British croquet, if you hit another ball and knock it out of bounds, you simply place that ball in one yard anywhere (by the imaginary yard line that runs all the way around the inside of the court) and *continue your play*. Again, this difference requires some different strategies.

In British croquet, only a rover can knock out another rover. Also, a "wired" ball (one that is unable to be hit because it is up against the wicket) can be lifted and placed on either baulk line, whereas in the American game it cannot be moved. Penalties are essentially the same in both games. You still should try to play in turn—though it's harder to go out of turn when you're playing the British game.

Let's begin a British game and then rush it [sic] along to a quick conclusion, simply as a way of illustrating a few more points. Let's say that Wendy's English cousin Harriet has arrived for a visit, with Charles, and you and Jill are going to try "their" game. Wendy's cousin is from London. She truly believes that *her* type of croquet game is the best. She has never even *heard* of American croquet, much less played it. She's very "proper" and polite. As is Charles, her fiancé. They have been engaged for seven years and Jill privately wonders, as does Wendy, whether they have kissed yet.

As your object is to set as many breaks (hit other balls and keep earning more strokes to advance you and your partner) as possible, you do not simply try to get through the first wicket as you begin. If you and Jill have won the toss and elected to play first (meaning first and third), the opponents get to choose their colors (blue and black). Jill goes first by placing her ball on the south (or "A") baulk and hitting it over to the right-hand side a good ways. Harriet then places her ball up the west side at some distance. Harriet's move is usually referred to as a "tice," meaning it is placed in such a way as to *entice* an opponent to try to hit it and, it is hoped, miss. You can now either go over by Jill and keep her ball and your ball together (is *this* the weekend you are determined to decide, once and for all, if you can really *be* a *team*?), or you can take a chance and try to go up and hit Harriet. You choose to go over by Jill (this ambivalence *has* to be resolved). Charles follows suit by going up and actually hitting Harriet. He then maneuvers to bring them both back and get himself through the wicket, then leaves himself almost where he is (just through the wicket) for Harriet to use when it is her turn. Very polite.

Jill now hits your ball hard, moving both her ball and yours together toward the first wicket, and so forth. This kind of breaks-oriented play (see full discussion of the important strategy of "breaks" in chapter 5) becomes very typical of the match, until, of course, you begin to get your balls aggressively entangled with the opposition's balls, at which time various other strategies come into play. In any event, you progress through the wickets in the same order, and then at the end you come through the sixth wicket with the stake at your back, turn around and proceed either to hit the stake or play as a rover ball. As it has been a long game, and Charles and Harriet do not seem to have read an American paper since arriving two weeks ago, and as they are not very interesting anyway, you have not really had much conversation. It has been a long and tedious game, made better only because you have been winning most of the time and indeed are enjoying beating them at "their" own game.

Roque

Every popular game spawns a few "deviant" offspring, games that are similar and yet different, games that are derived from the mother game but nevertheless are seen, variously, as both adventurous and unseemly offspring. In this sense, and without meaning to be unfair, roque is really a bastard ("golf croquet" is a little less of an upstart, but not *really* a croquet game so much as a warm-up, learning experience).

To be specific, roque was born in a defiant mode. In 1889 the British Croquet Association decided not to allow a certain kind of croquet mallet to be used. This mallet had a rubber tip on one end of the head and a metal or very hard surface at the other end. In a great show of inestimable petulance, Americans angered by this ruling decided to pick off two letters from the word "croquet"—a "c" from the front of the word (was this the rubber-tipped end?) and the "t" from the other end (the metal end?). The result spelled the word "roque" (rhymes with broke). This may be the first known case of consonant theft being used as a symbolic gesture to the world.

Once the word "croquet" had been ripped off at both ends, the Americans returned in a huff to their native land and developed the game of croquet under a new set of rules and with its new name. Roque is probably not a game that many of us will play. It is not even a game most of us would begin playing. Its life was not particularly distinguished, and, indeed, many people are still critical of the Americans who had such a hard time accepting the ruling of the British Croquet Association that triggered this international event.

Roque was played quite a bit in the United States at the turn of the century and, in fact, was included as an official sport in the 1904 St. Louis Olympics. That was the end of the game's Olympic voyage, however, and it is not likely to return to that forum in the future. Still, roque was played in the United States for some time and is still played today, though not very frequently and not in too many locales. *Its* "comeback," unlike *croquet's*, may lie only in the distant future.

O

Unlike croquet, roque is played on a court that is bounded on all four sides by a 12-inch-high cement wall. It doesn't even seem to be made in the same green mode. The roque court has, really, the appearance of a giant sandbox, for the dimensions of the enclosing rectangle are 30 feet by 60 feet. Roque is played with curious-looking short mallets, and when you play, you use the walls, just as if you were playing off the banks (side cushions) in a pool or billiards game (in this sense the relationship between croquet and billiards is, perhaps ironically, given greater clarity and historical continuity). Playing roque thus allows you to talk about going off the wall, while in "real" croquet we know this can never happen.

Roque has been popular for a variety of reasons, including the fact that during the Depression in the United States, the government had public works employees build a number of these strange-looking, cement-walled roque courts—not the grassy lawns of Victorian England, but nevertheless courts that could be built in a variety of locations. The course of the ball was different, particularly as bank shots were virtually necessary to negotiate certain wickets. The much shorter mallets were usually swung from the side with one hand.

Most books on croquet do not go into great detail about roque. This strikes me as wise. It is an interesting historical development,

O

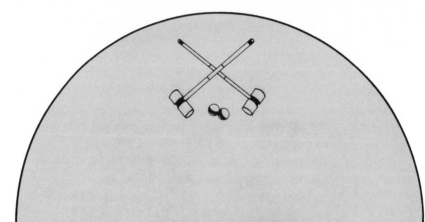

GOLF CROQUET

Golf croquet is something of an anomaly, a crossbreed, a curious invention of those who at some point decided to merge some of the system of golf with the equipment and practices of croquet. It is not a variation of croquet, as, say, American or Association croquet, but rather an entity in its own right, a game unto itself, one that croquet players can try a mallet at for diversion and even, some maintain, as an easy introduction to certain useful croquet shots.

To begin with, unlike croquet but like golf, the entire focus is on the next wicket to be made. An individual (or team) wins if he gets through the wicket in the least number of turns. Unlike golf, one does not talk in terms of "par" or "bogies," but the intent is similar. In croquet it is not the number of shots it takes you to advance that determines the winner but rather who finishes the course first. In golf croquet, in contrast, every player is trying to get through the same wicket. Players take their turns in the same order as in croquet (blue, red, black, and yellow) and balls are paired as partners in the same way. However, once, say, the black ball

○

has cleared the single wicket that everyone is aiming for, all is done and finished with that wicket and yellow, as the next player in turn, then has the first shot at the next wicket. Whoever goes through a simple majority of the wickets first wins. So it is like golf in being oriented toward a low number of strokes, but unlike golf because not everyone has to make the wicket—just the player who can get through it first. It is like croquet because you are using a croquet mallet and ball and making some similar shots, but unlike croquet in many respects, including the fact that in croquet every ball is trying to get through every wicket. So golf croquet is an odd duck at best. But it has its own popularity and followers and has even been encouraged as a good kind of precroquet activity for beginners.

When you play golf croquet you keep score by assigning a point to each team that gets *either* of its balls through the most wickets, with a total number of seven points. This is achieved by playing six wickets and then wicket number 3 if there is a three–three tie. The six-wicket layout is preferred.

During and after the Depression, roque, which is played with short-handled mallets, became popular and was played on WPA-built public courts. Painting by Paul Sample, as reprinted in *Life*. *Courtesy: New York Public Library Picture Collection.*

and no doubt the game had (and probably still has) its ardent devotees. The problem is, I have never met any. I have never even *seen*
anyone play roque, ask me about it, tell me about it, or even express
any particular awareness of it. So, rather than present a diagram of
the layout of the game, I will suggest you take a look at older books
on croquet or see the full discussion in the *Encyclopaedia Britannica* if
you want the details and the court dimensions, and so forth.

What does strike me as worth commenting on before leaving this
consonant-deprived creation, however, is the way its birth symboli-
cally represents the intensity of feelings that people can develop about
croquet. Imagine the depth of feeling, of pique, it would require to
object to a rule about a piece of equipment in a sport to the extent
that you would pick up your mallet and go home and refuse to play
any more. And then to form an entry in the *Olympics*! What if the
NBA changed the regulations about the size of a basketball? Can you
imagine anyone going off and creating a new game, maybe with three
instead of two baskets, and calling it "asketbal"? Or objecting to the
head of a golf club and thus creating a new game that you *could* play
with "your" kind of club, and calling the new game not golf but "ol"?
How about other new games like "ing-pon" (they lowered the net
and you'll show *them*), or "ock" (they said "no" to your thickness of
puck so you stole the "h" and the "y").

Only in the world of croquet, this evolving, maniacal, and ob-
sessive game/sport/recreation/leisure/pastime, could feelings rise to
such a piranhalike feeding frenzy as to result in banishing two con-
sonants from the game's own name. Even if you live in Owego, New
York, instead of Oswego, New York, you're only down *one* consonant.

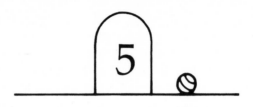

With Mallet Aforethought: Shots and Strategies

Beginning croquet players are probably curious about the title of this chapter. Why "shots"? "You swing your mallet and you hit your ball, right?" Actually, this *is* right, and even though there are some specific shots that it is good to understand and use, what you do is still always the same: You swing your mallet and you hit your ball. You always use your mallet to hit *your* ball. And you *never* use it to hit someone else's ball (or to assault another person, even Fred). You may hold your mallet beside you and swing it that way, or in front of you and swing it away from your body, starting somewhere to your rear (legs, of course, apart). But you want your shots to reflect cunning, to be fully effective in improving your position while simultaneously weakening your opponent's. In short, you really need to proceed with mallet aforethought.

Let's pause and give a little thought to the different ways you

○

Croquet has always been popular with men and women of all ages. The little girl pictured on the left seems as hypnotized as the others by the magnetic power of the stake. A nineteenth-century engraving.

O

can hold your mallet. I don't want to spend a lot of time on this because I believe it borders on being as subjective an element of the game as there is. For example, you can hold your mallet out to the side fully and swing it like a golf club. This is very satisfactory for those golfers who have trouble hitting a golf ball squarely. It is pretty easy to hit a croquet ball directly when using a golf-club grip.

Most people like to stand with their feet apart and swing the club up the middle; here there are differences as well, as you can stand with your feet parallel or with one foot placed farther to the rear. If you stand too far away from the ball you may not hit it as "cleanly" as you wish, and if you are on top of the ball you may chop down at it in a clumsy way. Only *you* can really decide how to address the ball (I always wonder why we talk about "addressing" a ball, except when we know where we wish to *send* it). The most important point about all of this is to be comfortable, relaxed, *at one with your mallet.* Join your mallet meditatively. Concentrate yourself into it, down the handle, into the head, into the color. Breathe deeply. Then strike with a sudden cobralike clarity and with just the right amount of force to achieve your goal: death to the enemy, or perhaps just a harsh wound.

Now, what *about* shots? In the first place, there are different ways to hit your ball for different results. The choice of shot has to be tied to your objective in the specific situation you are in, and at a specific point in the game. If, for example, you are beginning, it is easiest to stand between the stake and the first wicket and swing the mallet away from you very directly to send your ball through the first two wickets. That's a "shot" in itself, a direct and simple advancement of your ball to get through a wicket. Some people do nothing more than that for the rest of the game. A person who uses this approach is often considered to be (in the delicate language of croquet) an "Aunt Emma." This individual is avoiding any confrontation with other balls and is simply taking a nerd's-eye view of the game. It is important to learn how to make shots that will allow you to hit other balls, for this is the only way to win at croquet.

A second reason for knowing about shots is connected to the importance of mind-set. To walk out on a croquet lawn and ask dumb

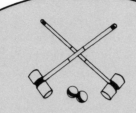

AUNT EMMA AND AUNT SALLY

Many croquet players know that the slang term for a slow methodical "safe" player who simply and quietly progresses from one wicket to the next without trying to hit other balls or take any risks is "Aunt Emma." One can be called worse, certainly, but how about being an "Aunt Sally"?

Apparently this label has been used for anyone treated abusively. Originally it referred to a woman's wooden head on a pole which was used in a game played at town fairs during the Middle Ages. People threw balls at her and tried to knock either a pipe out of her mouth or her head off completely. Being an Aunt Emma would *seem* easier to live with, so if you are a very conservative player, don't take too much offense if you get called an Aunt Emma; instead reply that you hope your antagonist becomes an Aunt Sally. He or she probably will not know what you mean, but it's a nice way to be mildly inflammatory without dealing with further repercussions. And if opponents still want to be difficult even after this wild and confusing retort, tell them they are "not worth a 'rush,' " meaning that had *they* lived in the Middle Ages, you would not have used rushes (grasses) either to cover their floor or to burn for their light, for they would not be guests worthy of such special consideration. Then rush their ball on the next move and do them in doubly, with wit and mallet.

questions like "Is it my turn yet?" is bad enough, but to be caught—indeed, exposed—in the state of *becoming* a player rather than having the presence of an actualized player can be demoralizing. If you don't know even the basic shots, you won't be bringing much to the party. On the other hand, if you can say, with a straight face and early in the game, "I think I'll try a jump shot" or "It's time for a rush," you will make it clear that you at least know how to talk about croquet even if you don't have great skill. Simply communicating your familiarity with shots is enough to make your opponents nervous. If you can get someone dumbly to ask you what a split shot is or how to rush, be sure to look amazed, aghast. Hold yourself, dilate your pupils (if you learned this earlier in life), be as dramatic as you can in indicating your supposed shock that someone might *not* know what you may have learned just yesterday (by reading this book, I hope).

Shots. The word itself evokes aggression and sexuality. A man's man takes a "shot" of whisky or fires a "shot" at someone either verbally or with a gun. "Go ahead, hit me with your best shot" is a cliché from many movie scenes. "Give it your best shot." "Take a shot at it." A shot is an opportunity that has been glamorized through the idiom. Croquet builds on the mystique of shothood even further by describing shots in ways that smack of war and athletic prowess—even though, to repeat, all you are doing is swinging your mallet to hit your ball.

Because in people's mind-sets croquet is not a "gentle" game at all, it needs a special language to cloak its essentially simple nature in a costume of rigor and combat. Thus we have, for example: cannon shot, drive shot, rush, split shot, stop shot, and the take-off shot. All connote vigor and combat. Heard out of context, do these terms quickly make you think of the gentle game of croquet? In any case, let me explain some of these shots and then discuss how they are used as part of your *strategy* (not to be confused with simply knowing and following the rules). Along the way, of course, we must bear in mind the psychology of the game; for language and practice are tied closely to psychological "warfare" as you play. Finally, bear in mind at the outset that there are two categories of shots in croquet. Sometimes you make a shot that involves hitting just your ball (single-ball shot); other times you are hitting your ball while it is touching another ball (double-ball shots).

Single-ball Shots

ROQUET

RUSH

CUT RUSH

STRAIGHT RUSH

LONG RUSH

SHORT RUSH

JUMP SHOT

The *roquet* is the basic shot of the game. When you make a roquet, you are hitting your ball so that it hits one of the other balls you are alive on, thereby giving you two extra strokes. The roquet shot may be likened to hitting the cue ball in a game of pool to make it hit another ball. Croquet follows the same approach, in that you need to line-up on the ball you wish to make your ball hit. *How* you do that, however, varies from one theory to another. Some suggest looking back and forth from your ball to the other ball and then carefully looking only at your ball as you make a nice steady stroke. The conventional wisdom is that if you look up too suddenly you will miss hitting the other ball. Personally I don't put too much faith in all this theory because everyone has a different "feeling" for just how to make one's ball hit another ball. You don't *have* to stand or stroke your ball in one way and one way only. As with the other shots we will discuss, practice is well worth it. The more experience you have in hitting your ball to make it hit another ball, the easier it becomes.

Here we should pause in our discussion of mind-set and consider risk/reward. Few things are more intimidating than the prospect of making a long-distance roquet. If you can hit your ball a great distance and have it hit another ball, you can gain a tremendous psychological "first-strike" advantage over your opponent. However, there is also the risk: It is not *easy* to hit a ball from a great distance. It's like making a very long putt on a golf green, except that the grass is usually longer in croquet. Still, it is worth trying occasionally, with bravado and confidence. It is particularly good to attempt a lengthy roquet shot when there are several balls close to each other—any one of which you would be happy to hit. Be sure not to announce in advance *which* of the balls you are trying to hit. If you are lucky (skillful, you imply) enough to hit one of the balls, make it clear through body language (my favorite: bend at the knee, swing your arm, and vigorously snap your fingers) that you just did exactly what you meant to do. There's no way anyone can prove that you got lucky (this holds true for all successfully made shots, and much of life generally, so *never* reveal your intention). Even if a mallet-headed opponent tries to assert how "lucky" you were, tell him he's wrong. It's that simple.

How hard you hit your ball is not merely a function of how far away the ball you are aiming at is but also what you want to happen to that ball. If you want to just jostle it, hit your ball lightly. If you want to *move* it a certain distance, you'll want to make a rush shot.

The *rush* is not a spurt of adrenaline. It is certainly not the response to taking a toke or trying crack. It is not being invited to join a sorority. There is no rush night—just another linguistically revved up croquet shot. When you make a roquet in such a way as to move the ball you are hitting a significant distance (meaning more than a jostle), you are making a rush shot. If you want to move the struck ball a long way you are making a *long rush*; if a short way—say less than several feet—a *short rush*. There are a few further variations, and of course more language.

The *cut rush* is a rush in which you want to send the struck ball off at an angle. People who have studied vectors in math will have an advantage in this, but it also helps to keep pool in mind as you play the angles. The *straight rush* is not a poker hand but a rush in which you want to move the struck ball straight away. These terms are fairly simple and describe your basic shots. You will make more rushes than virtually any other shot. Nevertheless, it's always a good ploy to step up to your ball and exclaim that you think you'll try a cut rush. People look at one another fearfully. You have their attention. Do it. *Make* that awesome cut rush.

When you want to put some forward "English" on your ball, hit it on the top (again just as in pool). In general, when you make rush shots, you should simply line up carefully on the ball you wish to hit and swing your mallet evenly, giving the head of the mallet a clear, pendulumlike, well-balanced motion and applying the appropriate amount of force for your objective. On a long rush you need to hit your ball harder than on a short rush, and so forth. And even on a cut rush, you have to make the same choice about how far you want to move the other ball, not simply consider the angle at which you want to be sent.

The *jump shot* is an intended attempt to make the ball jump (never a desired outcome in pool). When you execute a jump shot you strike your ball as far down on it as you can with a choppy motion, to get it to jump. Why? Well, of course it's more than a little satisfying to get your ball up off the ground for a change. After all, croquet can get pretty monotonous. More significantly, you use a jump shot because—guess what?—you want your ball to jump over something. Possibly a twig or some bird doo on the greensward, but *usually* over another ball, and sometimes even a wicket. If you want to go through a wicket and there is a ball sitting right in the wicket's "jaws" (another example of the dramatic language of croquet), you make a jump shot so that your ball can get right up over the other ball in a leap-frog sort of way, getting your ball through and leaving the other ball still wicketed.

If you want to take the other ball through the wicket as well, you don't make your ball jump quite so high. It will then just sort of crawl (all) over the other ball (who's raining on whose parade now?) and usually bring the other ball through the wicket. This has a rather sluggish tempo (more inchworm than panther), but it works. It's in the nature of croquet to have a jump shot, given the fact that the highest the ball may get off the ground is four or five inches. Say, now! Incidentally, in order to use jump shots to go through wickets, obviously your wickets must be two balls high. Therefore, if you have

O

a coat hanger in the set, or a wicket too deeply plunged into the earth, exchange it for this turn and get through with the jump shot. It can be a lot of fun before a game begins, especially with newcomers, to mumble (loudly) to your partner that you really hope you have the opportunity to make some jump shots. It really psyches people out if they don't know what a little deal this shot is.

One note of caution about jump shots. Because you are swinging up hard at the lower part of the ball, forcing it to jump as you pass on, you often plow your mallet head into the lawn. If your lawn already has lots of little rough spots and minipotholes on it, as most do, this will not matter. If you are on someone else's lawn, however, and it is perfectly groomed and maintained, be prepared to hear some pretty heavy-duty rhetoric as your opponent *explains* (snarls) to his partner that it is not *necessary* for the mallet to go into the lawn on a jump shot. Alternately, he may quietly walk over and pick up the divot you've dislodged, then fuss over it a little as he returns it to the place where—as his expression makes clear—it was unnecessarily dug up. If all of this irritates you, make sure to take another jump shot fairly soon!

Now we come to a difference between backyard croquet and the more official versions of the game, as outlined in chapter 4. In the home-grown variety, you may well play this way: When you make a roquet, that is, hit another ball you are "live" on, you can "send" it by placing your ball directly against the other ball, putting your foot on your own ball (my sister's bare toe-curling power haunts me to this day, as should be evident by now) and then hitting your ball. Your foot holds your ball where it is as the other ball is "sent" away. This, as anyone knows who has done it, is incredibly satisfying. It is difficult to think of more than one or two more satisfying moments in life, especially if you are sending someone who earlier sent you. Or, if you need the two extra strokes you have earned by hitting this other ball to advance, you may just leave the other ball sitting there, place your ball a mallet head's length away, and take your two strokes.

These basic choices are yours to make, no matter which game of croquet you are playing. However, I should at least make you aware of the fact that "real" croquet players, whether they eat quiche or

Even if their clothes are in touch with the times, nobody feels good when an opponent is in touch with one's ball—and about to send it! An art deco illustration from a 1915 French magazine.

not, tend to do neither of these things, except when they become emotional and are unable to resist sending a ball far away (which in backyard croquet actually seems to become a lot more important, certainly to pain-in-the-ass Fred, than making the wickets). Instead, after making a roquet, the croquet player decides to make a croquet shot.

Help? Yes, croquet is the name of the game. It is also the name of a stroke. It is also the name of a shot. A stroke is any swing of the mallet, whereas a shot refers to a particular type of swing for a particular outcome (for example, making the ball jump).

Double-ball Shots (Croquet Shots)

DRIVE SHOT

ROLL SHOT

STOP SHOT

87

SPLIT SHOT
TAKE-OFF SHOT
CANNON SHOT
PEEL SHOT

CROQUET

O

A *croquet shot* is one in which you strike your ball *while* it is in contact with another ball. Just as "roquet" means the principal generic single-ball shots, so "croquet" describes double-ball shots. When you make a croquet shot you still *hit only your* ball, but you *move* both your ball and the ball you have placed yours next to before you swing. The other ball is known as the croqueted ball, and you can make it go various places and distances depending on which type of croquet shot you make. Because the croquet shot is the basic shot of double-ball play, it naturally has variations that are represented as other shots. There are about as many double-ball shots as Henry VIII had wives, and a few of them even have some variations of their own. We will focus on the basic ones.

The *drive shot* is the most elementary double-ball shot. You simply place your ball directly behind the other ball and swing evenly. The result is that both balls are cleanly driven straight ahead and the second ball travels roughly three times as far as your ball. How hard you strike your ball thus determines where both balls end up (as is always the case), but the one-to-three distance ratio stays the same. Don't ask me why. I majored in English, not physics. Remember Harpo Marx's enthusiasm for making his drive shots with a golf swing, which could send both balls crashing through greenhouse windows.

The *roll shot*, as the name suggests, is a sweeping or rolling shot that makes both balls go just about the same distance, or roll *together* to the same point. To make a roll shot you swing down at the top of your ball and pointedly follow through with your swing so that the force of the follow-through makes your own ball keep traveling right along with the other ball. When you're on a roll, you can really feel it. Of course, *what* you feel depends on with whom you are rolling. If you are taking a partner along with you to keep the two of you

88

together in your progress in the game, it can have a very matrimonial and space-sharing dimension to it. If you are bringing the enemy along with you, it is likely that you have more sadistic purposes in mind for that ball later. So you may be with a wonderfully romantic traveling companion, or you may be like the sheriff on horseback bringing in the prisoner who is tied to a rope behind the horse. Either way, when you're on a roll it's pretty darned emotional, especially in this game.

The *stop shot* is one I love to think about because it gives me the picture (a false one, unfortunately) of saying the hell with the game, the mosquitoes are getting too bad, and announcing that this is my final shot. I am *stopping*, finis, *done!* The reality, alas, is that I am still in the game despite the mosquitoes. The stop shot is a double-ball shot intended to make the other ball travel and your own ball—guess what?—*stop* essentially where it is. You swing down hard at your ball and gouge (ideally not very much) into the lawn behind it with your mallet so that the impact of your strike makes the other ball take off, while the ground deadens the weight of the mallet's impact on your own ball. This is more or less like sending another ball by placing your foot on it; indeed, you can send the other ball a great distance, for typically it travels ten times as far as your own ball. This is one of those times in life that you do not want to follow through. Just stop your swing as you hit. With a little practice you can dig up a good part of your lawn.

The *split shot* is not a cracked or halved shot, nor is it a shot in need of psychological counseling (a *multiple* shot, however, might benefit from referral), but a variation of a pool shot. Basically, your goal in a split shot is to send your ball off at one angle and the other ball off at a different angle (therefore in a different direction). You "split" the total angle as you hit your ball, just as in pool. With a little practice you can get a good feeling for how to make the two balls travel quite consistently at the angles you want, while slowly learning how, for example, to leave your ball on the "right" (entering) side of a wicket and the other ball on the opposite side. You then can go through the wicket, hit the other ball again, and then make *another*

○

double-ball shot, and so forth. The key to a good split shot is being able to hit the ball exactly as you know it needs to be hit for the results you want.

The *take-off shot* has a name that, like the stop shot, brings forward some bizarre fantasies. You might think, for example, that the take-off shot allows you to leave the game and go home to watch television (about as much exercise is involved either way), or you might picture your ball not simply jumping but really "taking off," as an airplane. Fun, but wrong again, for the take-off shot is rather like the opposite of the stop shot. When you make a take-off shot you hit your ball at such an angle as to make it "take off" from the other ball, which, in turn, does not move very far at all. To make your ball take off and the other ball either hardly move or else travel just a short way, requires you to swing at your ball at almost a right angle to the other ball. But not quite a right angle. The other ball *must* move (jiggle) or the shot is null. Therefore, you must put just a little bit of an angle on it as you send your ball on its way—usually a good distance.

The *cannon shot* evokes my favorite fantasy: I get to shoot either myself or my croquet ball out of a cannon—at Steve or Wendy, perhaps, depending on how far it is into the summer. To me, the mere name of this shot stands for all that is machismo in the language of croquet. Here is this innocuous game of pushing balls around on the ground and yet it includes something called a heavy-duty *cannon* shot: As if the battlefield were physical rather than psychological, or as if you played in combat fatigues instead of Bermuda shorts. A cannon is, after all, a big gun. It is artillery. It is, in fact, also a hard straight serve in tennis and, it turns out, a somewhat complicated croquet shot that involves hitting your ball and another ball in such a way that the other ball goes on to hit yet *another* ball. Cannon shots are like "combination shots" in pool. You need to calculate the angle to make the second ball go where you have first determined *it* must go in order to hit the third ball at the angle you want *that* ball hit. Practicing cannon shots is fun, as the challenge of making these angles all work out is very satisfying.

The *peel shot*, to conclude, is not as slippery as all that. When you make a peel, you do not undress, but instead simply strike your ball in such a way as to make the other *hit* ball go through a wicket. If you make it go through two wickets (likely only at the two ends of course) you have made a double peel. If we add a double dip to the double ball, the split, and the peel, we'll be close to a very good dessert, or so it would appear.

Review Exercises

Try to complete the following with the name of a shot:

1. not slowly, but in a _____. rush
2. not a howitzer, but a _____. cannon
3. not to land, but to _____. take-off
4. not together, but _____. split
5. not to dive, but to _____. jump
6. not a start, but a _____. stop
7. not a biscuit, but a _____. roll
8. not a rind, but a _____. peel

If you scored all correct, you are probably a better and more knowledgeable croquet player than most, certainly than I. If you scored half right and half wrong you may be able to find the right partner yet. If you scored only two or three right, you may need therapy. If you could not get any right, I would like to meet you for a game of croquet, gentle or otherwise.

1. tootsie-_____. roll
2. _____-in movie. drive
3. _____-ball Aderly. cannon
4. _____ personality. split
5. _____ sign. stop
6. sorority _____. rush
7. _____-ing jacks. jump
8. banana _____. peel

One final point. In making the various shots described, realize that you must work on them, practice them. If you understand the shots—what they are and how they are intended to be made—you will be able very quickly to make most of them very well. The exception might be the cannon shot, which requires additional practice, though not, as I had first suspected, a village green. With a grasp of the shots—the arrows in the quiver as it were (and wickets having an archery of their own)—you are ready to think about *strategy*. How can you *use* these shots to best advantage? When does it make sense to use a roll as opposed to a stop shot? How can you make a split shot in such a way as to help you and your partner *and* create a problem for *both* of the opposing balls? Your goal, after all, is to win the game.

Strategies

The main strategy, of course, is to have a comprehensive mind-set that enables you and everyone else to be convinced that you are an outstanding croquet player. This can be communicated more easily than demonstrated. Once you are firm and self-possessed, there are some more literal kinds of strategies to know about. Strategy is where rules and shots meet: It is hoped that if you understand the rules and the shots, the strategies will come together almost like a third ball in a cannon.

Getting All the Breaks

In croquet there is one very important strategy and the rest follow from it: making breaks. In a "break" you use one or more balls besides your own ball to advance through at least more than one wicket. This translates into playing your ball in such a way as to keep at least one other ball near to you that you can "use," that is, that you can hit (= roquet) and thereby earn extra strokes. The more you can use this ball and other balls, the more you can keep coming alive on them and hitting them and the more you can keep earning extra strokes— some of which you use to get through the wickets and some of which you use to earn still more extra strokes. This will allow you to get through still more wickets and hit balls again and earn even more extra strokes. There is no limit on the number of breaks you can play. Just as one player can run the table in a pool game, so in croquet you can travel through all the wickets by making one break after another. But it requires skill *and* thought. In any case, having a live ball nearby is like being able to plug into a power charge over and over again. Or perhaps even putting your ball in a microwave.

Making a good break means positioning yourself in such a way that you make a roquet, then a croquet, get through a wicket, and then hit the ball once again. After this second roquet, you then croquet again, often with a roll that will take your ball and the other ball right up near the next wicket. Then the process repeats. You just can't do all this without using another ball. You need to keep hitting *some* other ball to get the extra strokes. "Extra strokes for aggressive folks" might be a good jingle to recite if things are going well and you are making the breaks successfully. And if someone caustically remarks, "Some people get all the breaks," simply reply, *"That's right!"*

The basic part of "breakmanship" is the so-called two-ball break, in which you use just your ball and one other to progress. This strategy calls for using combinations of single-ball and double-ball shots (read on). In the central pattern of play, you might hit the other ball, thereby earning two strokes. You can then do a roll to take the two balls over near the wicket. You still have a stroke left so you go through the wicket. This entitles you to another stroke, which you use to hit the other ball (as, having passed through a wicket, you are "alive" on it again). Now you again have two strokes.

Let's back up for a minute. After you have gone through the wicket and depending on where you left the other ball, now you may wish to hit the ball in such a way as to move both balls or have them stay where they are. Then, again depending on position, you will probably want to take the two balls on a roll shot to the next wicket. How far apart you make the two balls come to a stop will depend on which type of shot you select and, of course, on how much skill you have. But your obvious strategy is to be able to repeat the process of getting through the wicket with the next stroke, winning another stroke, then hitting the ball again.

More often than not you will need to make split shots, sending your ball to one side of a wicket (so that it's in position to go through on your next stroke) and the other ball to the other side. In this way you can, with just one ball, bring yourself and the other ball all the way along the course, clearing all the wickets and pegging out. Of course, if you make a mistake, the other ball will be able to use you, which is why if you can travel well ahead with your *partner* ball, you are better off than traveling with your opponent ball. If you travel with your partner you can try to bring him through the wickets with you, and he presents no threat if you miss. However, if you are using your opponent in this way, and you goof, he can use you to clear the entire course or, to be nasty, he can send you to a dank, musty corner at the opposite end. Just as you use breaks, so does the opposition. This is an important strategy to try: While you make breaks, prevent your opponent from doing so. Try to keep his balls separated whenever you can, and try not to leave your ball too near him for him to use you.

Mastering the two-ball break is the key to successful competitive croquet. Not surprisingly, you can become even *more* competitive and more successful if you can play "three-ball breaks" or even "four-ball breaks." The principles are the same. Your general strategy is to use not one but several other balls to advance your ball along the course. By having several balls together, you can use one (say you are dead on the first) to win extra strokes when otherwise you would have to stop. With the extra strokes and perhaps a split shot, you can then get through the wicket, hit another ball or two, use one shot to advance, say, one ball up to the area of the next wicket, then use a roll to take your ball and a second ball up to the same general location. Just bear in mind that you can never have more than two strokes remaining. You can earn two new strokes as many times as you want, but you never have more than two to play. A deadness board, which helps keep track of the balls on which you are "dead," becomes very helpful when you (and others) are playing a game based on three-ball and four-ball breaks.

One of the important points about making breaks is that you and your partner must do some strategizing. It *is* like chess in the sense that you have to think through "if I do *X*, then she will do *Y*" types of sequences. If you are playing multiball breaks and the balls are clustered, the opposition will play a turn before you have another turn. As simple as this may seem, it needs to be underscored, for couples often mistakenly plan as if one of them will immediately follow the other's turn. Meanwhile, between their turns, an opposing player might clear all the wickets of the course, keeping all the balls with him but with only *his* ball going through the wickets. The cumulative impact of having your ball dragged along by an opponent, simply to be *used*, can really get you down. It is here that many "friendly" or "gentle" games of croquet can get very nasty. The entire time you are being used, you are thinking about your need to go back and get through the wickets. The longer you are delayed, the lousier you feel. There are times when you ask if you will *ever* get another turn. If you *do* have a lot of time on your hands, however, consider falling in love!

One redeeming dimension of this situation is that you can get some diverting mental stress going between members of the opposing team in the following way: Encourage the opponent—let's say on her turn—to try to set up a three-ball break plan. As she advances herself by using not only one opponent's ball but also her partner's ball, the partner will *have* to begin wondering why he and you are being treated in the same way. Is her ego and stardom drive so great that she doesn't care more about her partner's ball than the opponent's? Of course, if she is playing three-ball breaks while also getting her partner through the wickets, the situation changes. Now you might comment on how he can't do it alone, how he *needs* her, how *dependent* on her he is, how he would never be this far along in the game (or in life) if it were not for her. Enough of this talk will finally make him feel totally worthless in his own right. And that is a very good—though perhaps nihilistic—strategy.

When you become the controlling player of three-ball breaks, you have the ability to send one or two balls to different places to be used later. It is not unlike the way a spider spins a cocoon around another creature to store it for food to be eaten later. You can use one ball right away to get the extra strokes, then get onto another, send it near a wicket that is several ahead of you but that will make it easy for you to stop and hit along your way, and thus insure your ability to travel a fairly long distance without even having to make a single hard roquet. Here again, you will want to confer with your partner, on the one hand, and, on the other hand, do everything you can to make the other two players feel a sense of hopelessness. You might even want to recite, just as a diversion, Tennyson's lines that make use of the word "break," not that they have anything to do with the situation, but just to make your opponents uneasy:

> *Break, break, break*
> *On thy cold gray stones, O Sea!*
> *And I would that my tongue could utter*
> *The thoughts that arise in me.*

Such a mysterious recitation of poetry can slowly begin to force the opponents to become detached from reality. They will begin to feel that they are not really there at all, that those are not really their balls being used as you rack up your victory. One of them may begin talking openly about vacation plans for later in the summer. That's just fine—because a few weeks later when you see each other in the city, it will all come back. They *will* remember how badly they lost. It will make it harder for them to play well the next time. The series of breaks you rack up now may help you keep the upper hand for years. Then, when your child is not accepted at a college of his or her choice and their child is, you will have something to cling to. It will help.

So is that it? Breaks, breaks, breaks?

Well, yes and no. Breaks *are* the main strategy to use to win croquet. After mind-set, breaks are everything. Still, there are a few other ideas to keep in mind. Just as in pool and billiards you give a lot of thought (recall Emerson's warning, "Beware when the great God lets loose a thinker on this planet") to where to "leave" your ball, so should you think about "leaves" in croquet. When you know it is your last stroke and that you are not going to be able to hit a live ball or get through a wicket, your only remaining decision is where to leave your ball. Sometimes, of course, your ball is left where it is because you failed to hit another ball or to get through a wicket and that was the chance you took. But if you have any power to decide, then you should think about where you prefer to leave your ball. Your decision should be based on the answers to a simple set of questions. What's the *worst* place for me to be from the opponent's point of view? Where's the *best* place for me to be from my partner's point of view? (Or, if playing singles, from the point of view of my other ball, which I will be playing next.) The answer to the first of these questions should take precedence because the opponent has the next turn. When taking a shot in an attempt to hit another ball, you may wish deliberately to overshoot, for example, knowing that if you miss, you will be leaving your ball in a place where it may be hard for another ball (such as the one you missed) to hit.

Leave yourself behind a wicket so an opponent can't get at you. Leave yourself over by the edge of the boundary so that he may go out of bounds by trying to hit you (see "tice" in the glossary). Leave yourself *anywhere* you can that will make it less likely for him to be able to use you (there is something relevant to corporate culture in this). If you can accomplish this while at the same time making it at least somewhat likely that your partner *will* be able to use you on his next turn, that is your best strategy.

Finally, when you get toward the end of the game, remember that you and your partner both need to peg out for you to win. It is usually fairly obvious at what point you should take yourself out. There is, in fact, often a gamble: If you stay in the game for your partner's sake, you may be used by the opponent, and thereby you will really have stayed in for the enemy's sake. Ditto, if you go out for the opponent's sake; you may weaken your partner's ability to finish the game. The main thing to bear in mind is not to end just for the sake of ending (no matter how late or dark it is, or fed up you are), but to end in the most *strategic* way. That peg can be very tempting. After all, it's the end of the line, the top of the mountain,

○

the golden fleece. But as Dylan Thomas said about getting ready to die—and you are finally *really* "dead" and out of the game once you hit the peg—"do not go gentle into that good night." Go when it is best not just for you but for your partner. That makes the most sense, and you may even have to make the hard choice to take out your partner, send him to the stake, before yourself, knowing that if you don't, your team will lose. If an opponent reaches the point where he is about to drive his partner's ball into the stake, make a lot of comments about how he is trying to kill her—*kill*, coldbloodedly— incredible. If that can be made to appear like a truly despicable thing, you may just get that extra turn—which will allow you to do that same despicable thing. And win. And such is the nature of the gentle game of croquet.

6

Croquet for Two: Tips on Courtship

It would be easy in thinking through the rules, dynamics, shots, and strategies of croquet to overlook the fact that it is, in an almost nostalgically primitive sort of way, a wonderful game for two people to play. And not just in the sense of standard *tournament* singles matches where two opponents each play two balls. Therefore, this short chapter is intended to serve as a reminder that *two* people, at any level of formality, can have a very special sort of experience in playing croquet, and in doing so can very rapidly build not only skill but familiarity.

While intense yet uplifting rivalries build up between couples—especially where comparisons of other kinds (money, success, kids' accomplishments, and so forth) loom in the wings—croquet for two people has a kind of privacy and blissfulness about it. It is almost like swimming nude on a deserted beach. (I said *almost*.) It has ele-

Making the right moves in croquet
is important even in between
turns. Sheet music cover, litho-
graph by F. H. Carter after a
drawing by S. S. Frizzell, 1866.
*Courtesy: The American Antiquarian
Society.*

ments of courtship in the eyes of some, particularly because it is a
progressive game, with the excitement mounting the closer you get
to the end. As a game for two, croquet provides, minimally, a kind
of mental sanctuary. For you and your friend, partner, or spouse (you
might have all three in one) to go out into the backyard and play a
game by yourselves is a relaxing and very upbeat way to spend the
end of the day (even *one* couple rarely plays croquet in the *morning*).

Croquet for two is a bit different from any other sport because
each of you plays two different balls. Even in bowling you wait for
"your" (one and only) ball to return and then you roll it again. In a
chess game, you move one of many pieces, then the opponent moves
one of his. In tennis, you hit the ball, the opponent hits the ball. Ditto

Ping-Pong. But in croquet, you hit a ball, the opponent hits a ball, you then hit *another* ball and the opponent *also* hits *another* ball. The mere concept of controlling two different balls at once—which is how all singles games are played officially and in tournament—gives you a heady psychological feeling. At times you even begin to feel that you have finally cloned yourself successfully. With two of you out on the lawn, if one of "you" screws up, the other comes to your rescue. There is no fear that you will disappoint your partner. You *are* your partner, as hermaphroditic as a worm. It is as if you have full control over your life to a degree that you may never have in any other arena. The result is that you can make quiet trade-offs with your opponent. "Sure, go ahead and take that shot over. I know you didn't mean to hit the wrong ball," you might say, and in all likelihood the favor will be returned. When you and a friend play a game by yourselves, there is no one else watching or judging. And there is a peacefulness in learning the rules quietly; you can recall the thought we all have had that Emerson so well expressed: "I like the silent church before the service begins, better than any preaching." In a way, an informal game of croquet for two (*no* one else is watching) *is* like being in a church before things get going. As clonal antibodies or amused hermaphrodites, who's to know?

This is not to say that croquet games with actual partners are not great fun, because they are. Rather, the point is simply to remember that as a game for two people, croquet offers some special moments of joy. And, if you are a beginning player, playing with just one other person will allow you to learn from your mistakes without feeling self-conscious—and you can quote Oscar Wilde to yourself: "Experience is the name everyone gives to their mistakes."

You must learn early on that it is important to keep your two balls together so that you can make breaks successfully. It is *very* tempting to want to advance one of your balls as far along the course as you can. It can give you a feeling that at least your better half (and I mean *your*) is "getting out in front." Usually this is a false feeling. Even if you manage to get one of your balls several wickets ahead, if your opponent is traveling as a "team," he is likely to overtake you.

○

It is easy to overlook the fact that once your two balls are too far apart, they cannot use each other to make breaks and advance. If you are racing along with one ball, having made some breaks off the opponent's balls, and leaving your other ball behind, eventually you will pay the price loneliness exacts in the competition of croquet (and become an "Aunt Emma" while you are at it). For the same reason that croquet is a very slow game when you and your opponent each play only one ball, so too it becomes slow for *you* if your two balls cannot be advanced together.

When you play with two balls you begin by flipping a coin, as always. One side takes the blue and black balls and one side takes the red and yellow. You follow the order of the colors on the stake. When playing with just one opponent, with each playing two balls, it is important to check with the stake consistently and from the very beginning, as it is easy to forget which ball you played last. In fact, you can even find yourself thinking that it would be easier to play just one color. By using the stake you will avoid having your memory collide with your opponent's.

Split shots are very helpful for sending your two balls into places where they can be easily used. It makes good sense for you to stop and consciously try to slow down the ball that wants to get out ahead. So, for example, after the game has begun and your first ball has gone through the first two wickets, you can go over to the third wicket. If you get through it, instead of coming all the way out to the middle of the lawn for the center wicket (assuming a nine-wicket game), stay nearby the third wicket so that your other ball will be able to use the first one to get through the third wicket. And so forth. It takes concentration to focus on what is likely to develop over several turns of play. And whether you and your friend have decided to make it a truly "friendly" game is an issue. If you are in the mood for a really pleasant game, it is fun simply to agree that your principal purpose will be to advance your two balls, and not to wreak injury on the opponent—until the very end of the game. It must be understood that in the final analysis, when you are both nearing the end, you may have to play truly "against" your opponent rather than simply "for" yourself. This is because *somebody* has to take the initiative to win. It need not be horrible, but you do want to win, even if it has generally been a "gentle" game.

Croquet for two played with two balls offers seemingly endless possibilities. For example, if you do have trouble keeping your two balls together, the odds are that the opponent is trying to keep his or her balls together. Thus you can set out for the *two* of them and increase your odds of making breaks off both of the opponent's balls. If you then get through a wicket, you are "live" on both of them and can turn around and make breaks off both of them again. Furthermore, in advancing your two balls, you will find yourself making a lot of roll shots.

It can be more satisfying, perhaps in a narcissistic way, to do something to assist yourself rather than to assist a partner. You are the direct beneficiary of your generous nature. It is like being able to inherit in your own will, and indeed when you are alternating playing two balls you are able to satisfy any number of fantasies, and principally, of course, the time-honored reverie (Freud aside) that you are two different people. I wouldn't go so far as to recommend thinking of one ball as ego and one as id, but one minute you can say, "Ah, my turn, I'm taking my blue ball through," while a moment later you are saying "My turn, I'm black now." You begin to believe that you really are two players. And that leads to another wonderful aspect of croquet for two—you don't have to wait very long for your turn. You can set down your glass and never see it until the end of the game because you are lining up one ball or another almost all of the time.

Finally, there is something very special about playing croquet with just one other person. You are performing a kind of *pas de deux* in an outdoor ballet, but with no audience. In fact, when you play "just the two of you" you are practicing what you know in a secure and supportive environment. There are no guffaws. No one goes crazy if you dig up some of the lawn or turn your mallet sideways to hit the ball because you can't swing the mallet "with the wicket where it is" (you exclaim as if it had just been put down in front of you).

When you are responsible for half the balls on the lawn you find the learning process intensified and you become rapidly sensitive to the types of shots and the importance of making breaks to advance the pair of balls you are playing as a "team." For novices, croquet for two is hard to beat, and for those who enjoy playing longer, it provides maximum playing time. Either way, you win. Singles croquet is still not like singles badminton, however, in which it has been claimed that a player runs more than a halfback during a football game. Croquet for two has the potential to afford you more breaks in a late afternoon than you might otherwise see in a summer. It is fun and offers just the slightest feeling that you are getting away with something.

There are a few tips to keep in mind when first learning to play croquet for two. Here are several that emerged when I recently played a game with Dave, a friend in Michigan. He had played backyard croquet before, but never with each player playing two balls. Dave's an aerobic type and runs seven to eight miles daily, so we had to begin with some adjustment therapies to eliminate his initial guilt about engaging in a sport that does *nothing* for you physically.

When Dave had earned two strokes and needed to go over and get in front of a side wicket, with the intention of coming through and hitting his other ball (which had already cleared the wicket) on the other side, he neglected to think about what angle he wanted to come through at to best position himself for hitting the other ball. If, for example, the ball is directly on the other side of the wicket, framed at right angles, you might want your first shot to bring your ball directly opposite it on the other side of the wicket. You can simply go through and then line up the balls to take them along. However, if the ball on the other side of the wicket is closer to the center of the course, then you want your first shot to go a bit *past* the front of the wicket, in other words, "overshoot it" somewhat. Then when you come through the wicket on your second shot you and the other ball will both *already* be heading in the right direction before you even take another shot. Alternatively, if the ball you plan to hit after coming through the wicket is closer to the boundary, farther away from the center, you will want your first shot to stop short of the wicket. Again, as you go through the wicket, you will be doing so at an angle to hit the opposite ball as you come through.

When first playing any game of croquet, it is very easy to over-concentrate on getting through a wicket, when you also need to concentrate on getting into position to go through a wicket *at the most advantageous angle.* This is particularly important in two-person croquet because you are controlling two balls, and you always want to make it as easy as possible for *each* ball to be going through wickets *and* be getting as close to each other as possible. The same principle applies, Dave quickly learned, when positioning the ball in front of the wicket to come through it at the best angle to come toward the next wicket. As you are often coming in and out from the sides of the center in croquet, this is very important. Dave found that he could simply draw a line in his head from his ball to the wicket to the spot on the other side of the wicket he wished to be. When first beginning, however, he had, in effect, been wasting a shot by just getting through a wicket, then having to use the next shot to get to where he could have been on coming through the wicket.

Dave also asked whether he could send both of my balls. The answer is yes; as long as you are alive on a ball, you can hit it. Once you have hit it, you can follow any one of a number of options, including sending several successively.

Dave was quick to learn the advantage of keeping his two balls together. He also had to learn to make choices, not to just go through the nearest progressive wicket without thinking about what he as well as what *I* would do next. For even though what the other person will do next (and remember, in two-player, two-ball croquet, to be sure which *ball* he will next play) will depend, in varying degrees, on what you do next, so it must be thought through in advance (which is why so many players compare croquet to chess).

As a beginning player of this game, Dave had to overcome the desire to use a shot to "injure" me whenever he could instead of advancing himself, possibly getting through several wickets, and *then* considering how to relocate me to a worse place (ideally through a split shot). A beginning player should resist almost automatically

○

worrying about inconveniencing the other person and *first* advance his own balls, keeping them together, *then* get around to hanging up the other person. If you concentrate on the other person's balls, you may simply be spinning your wheels without advancing yourself in the course, which after all is the primary objective (despite the fun in fouling up the other person). More often than not, in two-person croquet, an experienced player can accomplish a great deal. A beginning player needs to realize this quickly and "think big" about how much he can accomplish in a single turn by keeping his balls together and making two- and three-ball breaks.

When you have learned to play two-person, two-ball croquet and are teaching someone else, it is productive to share some of the basic strategies, at least for the first half of the game. It will make the game better if the other player learns the best strategies. At a certain point, however, it will suddenly dawn on you, as it did in my game with quick-study Dave, that the person you are explaining everything to has not only learned well but in fact is on his way to beating you. When I saw Dave making some long roquets and proceeding to get both his balls through a wicket when playing one ball, well, that's when I stopped being nice and went after him. I had been saying that this was a "friendly" game; when he reminded me of that after I relocated his blue ball to the other end of the court, I had to respond, "Friendly doesn't mean letting you win!"

Within five minutes I watched Dave completely screw up the position of both of my balls. And he was grinning from ear to ear. He continued on his way. Smiling and laughing. Smug. A real pain in the ass. Now *he* should meet Fred. In the final minute I won, but only by a hair. I certainly did not let on to Dave that the game could have gone either way, that he might have won. Experience should have some premium, after all, and as he was so eager to play again, I figured he was into it now and would probably be beating me soon enough. Probably regularly. By the next day Dave was explaining to *me* that if you stood forward over your ball more fully and pulled the mallet farther back, you could make a better jump shot. As he demonstrated it, I wondered how long he had been secretly practicing

O

between games. The main thing is that he was enjoying the game so much and even calling it addictive.

Playing croquet for two with friends, with either six or nine wickets, will prepare you well for tournament singles play where each player always plays two balls. It is a wonderful, active, and very competitive game. It also can serve as an excellent form of courtship when you want to win Jill over (for the umpteenth time).

Croquet for Two:
Tips on Courtship

O

ν·

Sex and Croquet: Believe It!

There is no question in my mind, nor in at least some others, that some of the charismatic staying power of croquet, its magnetism, is bound up with sex. While croquet is not exactly an outright challenge to have the right stuff or the best stuff, it's not a game for the romantically chicken-hearted either. There are numerous ways to flirt, stalk, and entice, and more than a few ways to hit on one another.

Numerous writers and croquet historians have documented ways in which croquet has reflected the sexual mores of the age. At times the game has been seen as almost asexual and boringly polite and at other times as a lewd and lascivious set of behaviors, an excuse for men and women to cavort together like sheep in an open green field.

In "The Immorality of Croquet," for example, an 1898 article that has been referred to by a number of croquet writers and which appeared in a Boston magazine entitled *Living Age*, the author worried openly and fretfully about the sexuality and bestiality inherent in croquet:

> the brute beast which underlies the thin polish of civilization is unchained; goaded to fury by each corrosive click of the croquet balls . . . the hoop, which beckons so temptingly and guilelessly from its carpet of green sward to cool and quiet croquet, is the gaping jaws of Hades. Who takes the mallet in his hand has grasped vice; and who passes through the treacherous wire portal leaves virtue, honor, and charity behind.

O

This seemingly satiric but, in fact, earnest expression of fear regarding croquet's immoral potential underscores rather dramatically, if clumsily, the inherent sexuality of the game. The sex *is* there, to be sure, but, of course, one cannot let it carry the day.

While today relatively few people debate the morality of croquet (there being more accessible arenas for controversy, such as the merits of different techniques for making a good jump shot or the best bracelets, sunglasses, and haircut to sport for tournament play), there is nevertheless an ongoing acknowledgment of the game's sexiness. One needs only to look at the "croquet marketing" of several products in recent years to find evidence of a sexuality that has been understood since the game began.

The Maidenform Bra woman, for example, always wearing only panties and her bra, appeared with a girlfriend, who wore a slip, both smiling and holding croquet mallets. With the usual slogan, "You never know where she'll turn up," the ad presents the two women on a croquet court. Behind them a handsome man, dressed in traditional white, is lining up his mallet on a ball. We are given the sense that in croquet men and women are intimately connected; women, in particular, learn that if they wear the right bra when they play croquet, more romance will come their way.

More recently Revlon launched a new Ultima II springtime color collection entitled "Croquet." In a discussion with advertising executives at Revlon, I learned that such a campaign results from a creative

Revlon chose croquet to market its new line of Ultima II cosmetics. Shot in Palm Beach, the ad catches the underlying mystique of romance and sexuality inherent in a good game of croquet. *Courtesy: Revlon.*

group going off on a retreat to develop a "shade theme"; a decision to go with croquet clearly reflected Revlon's usual outstanding creativity and ability to blend romance and healthy upscale living into an attractive, sociologically relevant campaign or package. In the ad, super-model Kim Alexis, who *is* stunning, wears a set of colors that are sensual and lush and which have been given names to match. Bent just right at the knee and crouched over a croquet ball, Kim smiles at the audience (we have to see her cosmetics, after all, for this is a shady business, and making the shot is clearly only secondary) over her mallet while men, once again dressed in white, stand around her in various positions. Revlon shot the ad in Palm Beach, a location that represents one of several particularly royal ways for American croquet players.

The Revlon ad has both romance and sex appeal, and captures the very life that flows from the colors of a croquet game, with the fertile greens and the virginal whites setting off the brightly colored designer jacket that helps bring it all together. Women are being told by this advertisement that wearing Croquet Ultima II should brighten their lives; it might also bring them to a croquet lawn like the one pictured. You too might well meet one of those presumably wonderful men standing around ogling Kim. In some unstated way, innocence and experience seem to come together.

In less dramatic ways, various ad campaigns and window treatments regularly depict men and women together in the "right" clothing as they hold the best mallets and stand near solid bright balls and heavy white wickets. Even in 1928 croquet scenes "marketed" wooden fences in this way! Bullocks Wilshire advertised wool—*cool* wool, that is—for fashionable clothing under a slogan "fast track wools" in a 1987 full-page ad in *Vogue* depicting an attractive woman jumping for joy almost orgasmically on a croquet court after her ball, in the foreground, has presumably just cleared a wicket (one doubts she would be airbone with joy if her ball had completely bypassed the wicket). It is clearly meant to be a moment of consummation and ecstasy.

Nikon is marketing a new camera, the Nikon One-Touch, by showing a great picture just taken—three generations of croquet players pause on the croquet court, several with drinks in hand. The good life, the picture seems to imply, as represented by croquet, will be that much closer to you with a good camera. From Brooks Brothers to Walt Disney, croquet is used in marketing and merchandising, and at least as often as not, sex and/or romance are part of the campaign.

Where does the sex come from? In part, it has to do with the fact that croquet is a game for both sexes to "play" together. Ironically, it was on this basis that many Victorians first applauded the game. As men and women began to appear to enjoy it too much, however, the tide turned against them temporarily, resulting in diatribes such as the one in Boston in 1898. It is not hard to speculate a bit further on the psychological dimensions of the sexuality of the game.

In Freudian terms, the mere idea of swinging long hard mallets

○

Croquet has been at the cornerstone of numerous marketing campaigns, including this one for fences, from a 1928 copy of *Country Life* magazine. *Courtesy: New York Public Library Picture Collection.*

to knock balls through inverted U-shaped hoops, now wickets, places in motion a set of elements with sexual associations. Furthermore, passing through a wicket, in both backyard croquet and American croquet, gives you new life; your balls become dead temporarily and then regain potency through a wicket rite of passage. That women get to swing something (*anything*) between *their* legs brings you up against Freudian theories of penis envy. Players get to deaden other balls, and these "smacks" (!) of castration underscore the equation of sex and power inherent in the rules. If you are alive on someone's ball, it is, after all, fair game to be pursued.

For men and women there is possibly even a faint promiscuity about passing through one wicket after another. The wickets are all the same . . . and yet, there is something different about going through each one. That the game is progressive, building in excitement as you continue to play, right up until you finally "peg out" (read *climax*), is worthy of thought, as is the whole sense of doing the same thing in different ways, always sensitive to your partner's needs.

And it is the partnership component of the game that provides the basis for a sexual bond. You play quite frequently with your significant other, and how both of you treat one another typically reveals the nature of your relationship. There is a bonding that takes place, and to win, you and your partner have to peg out as close together as possible. The progressive, building motions leading up to this point become a sustained courtship. Croquet allows for rhythms of flirtation, encounter, pursuit, death and rebirth, sex-role exchange—the variables seem endless. Thus it is not surprising that makers of bras and cosmetics try to build on the same underlying sensuality that has been perceived from the game's earliest origins, and which while sometimes attacked and sometimes celebrated, has always been either overtly or covertly recognized. You'll never find the same thing in horseshoes . . . although getting around *that* vertical peg for a "ringer" may be worth another author's ruminations.

Heightened awareness of the inherent sexuality in croquet may well lead to still further commercial exploitation. Just as a number of marketing and advertising campaigns have been based on croquet sex, so too we may soon have movies and musicals that take the sexuality still further. I myself am beginning to think about a comic, sexy movie to be entitled *Mallety D'Amour* in which a chorus line of sexily dressed wicked wickets prance around in brightly colored short skirts, while men (some perhaps corpulent) are dressed as balls and keep getting down and "rolling" between the wickets' legs. At first I thought my hero would be Rover, but now I've settled on a guy with real macho swagger: Mr. Stake (*"What a stake,"* everyone will say). The heroine will be an innocent young woman, Miss Wicket, who wanders unknowingly onto a croquet court in the darkness of the early evening, only to discover the seething passion and brothel-like atmosphere that takes over the court once most of the players have departed. There will be no castrating Queen of Hearts running around saying "Off with their heads," but instead the swagger and

One wonders whether onlookers here are interested in the shot this lovely lady is about to make or in her daringly raised hemline. A nineteenth-century illustration by C. G. Bush. *Courtesy: New York Public Library Picture Collection.*

bravado of Mr. Stake, whose solid, colorful charm is too much for our heroine to resist.

The fantasies I have that take off from the basic sexuality of croquet are surely not that unusual. At a subconscious level this game fairly reeks of sex. Certainly sexual encounters are themselves "gentle but wicket," and courtship and ravishment go hand in hand.

Take, for example, a poem from the late 1860s, a decade in which new women's fashions were beginning to reveal a bit of the foot. "The Croquet Queen, A Warning to Croquetters Against Coquettes," was first published by Reid in 1869 and reprinted in David Curry's book on croquet:

Her figure was faultless—nor tall, nor petite—
Her skirt barely touched the top lace of her boot;

I've seen in my time some remarkable feet,
But never one equalling that little foot,
Its tournure *was perfect, from ankle to toe—*
Praxiteles ne'er had such model for art—
No arrow so sharp ever shot Cupid's bow;
When poised on the ball it seemed pressing
    your heart!

In these few lines we move from the slightly raised skirt to the glimpse of the ankle, as the obsession of the poet brings him up against love that can hardly be contained. From footing the ball to foot fetish in one swift stroke of the pen!

One can retreat to the notion that people probably can, if they want to, find sex in just about everything. Maybe that is simply part of our normal quest for a stimulating life. Still, the fact that croquet is a *slow* sport gives it a greater sexiness than, say, running or swimming. If you are running or swimming vigorously with someone of the opposite sex, you *may* feel some sexual charges before and after, but *during*? Not likely. Croquet, on the other hand, draws down no estrogen. In fact, hormonally it's probably almost inert.

Standing around in a mixed company croquet game for a long time between shots, you can either be a voyeur, watching what everyone else is doing, or a quasi-lecherous adviser to any one of a number of other players. You have time to kill, and flirtation and romance are logical time-fillers. When you play croquet, you are often just sort of, you know, *hanging out*, so of course with people of both sexes present, something is likely to happen. As in movies like *Dr. Zhivago*, where the bitter cold virtually forces attractive strangers to clasp together in embraces to keep warm (alas, this has not yet happened to me on the Metro-North run from New Haven to New York), so in croquet, boredom and idleness stimulate participants into at least imagined passion—with hopes for later conversion to the real thing. And if you've got the right stuff, why not *be* Mr. Stake?

There are some pretty sexy moves in croquet besides the moves people put on each other. For example, let's assume you are a woman and your male partner is really into getting his stroke just right before he swings. He stands there typically with his legs apart and slowly, with two hands, swings his mallet back and forth as his eyes (possibly yours as well) flash from the general area of his crotch, to his ball, to his target. Like a rhythmic drum player, the throbbing grows until finally he takes his shot and he sighs (you may too).

Or let's say you're a man and your woman partner wants to place her ball just right. She bends down and places it next to the other ball. But when she stands up, her ball edges back so it is no longer touching the other one. Over she bends, again. It might require four trys. It's not that you're weird or anything, but you cannot help but notice her bending over repeatedly and, to some extent, you may find yourself stimulated. The Mr. Stake in you comes powerfully forward. By the time it's your turn to play you can hardly restrain yourself.

There is, furthermore, a boldness in the woman's movements on a croquet court that derives from the fact that she is required to make all the same moves as the man. Men secretly are supposed to like women to be at least as aggressive and maybe more so when it comes to sex. So women get to participate as equals, and men can, without saying so, happily accept this equality without compromising their own masculinity. Women get to feel just a bit "wicket," so when Miss Wicket and Mr. Stake really get it going, the sex is overwhelming. Just consider, too, that the ultimate in the game is to get to be an aptly named rover, able to travel around at will to visit all other balls, completely alive at all times. Because deadness is not applicable to a rover, the ball operates, really, free of a need for protection or restraint.

Certainly the language of croquet is supercharged with sexual connotations. Flipping through the glossary will quickly sensitize you to this—a drive shot, a rush, a roll, even *stroking* in *any* way, involves you linguistically in some sort of a passionate exchange.

There is, beyond doubt, a definite *naughtiness* about croquet. We don't do a lot with "naughty" these days, but our childhood interest in testing our limits, in going "out of bounds," never really disappears. Naughty means adventurous, really, and being naughty provides a sense of allowing some of our evil a teasing presence as opposed to a predominant one. Naughty lies behind flirtation. Naughty can be expressed by hitting another player's ball out of bounds, just sort of being perverse about it. Naughty can be cheating by going out of turn, just to see if you can get away with it. Read unfaithful. Naughty is foreplay for the *big* deed of pegging out together in the end. Naughty is when the wicket witch of the east meets the wicket witch of the west. Naughty is humorous but nevertheless a sexually stimulating activity, and croquet provides you with lots of opportunities.

For example, when two couples play and there is (be honest) a quietly understood degree of attraction across the couples, well, it might be hard to split one partner off to be with her (or him) at or after dinner, but on the croquet court, it's pretty easy. For one thing, you have every right to go after your friend's partner's ball and take the ball (and your friend's partner) with you wherever you want. It's sort of like eloping with a friend's spouse, and once *you* are both gone, well, there he is with *your* spouse, and nature being the way it is, things progress. This is understood about croquet—that partnerships get challenged, partners get split up (sometimes for the whole game), new pairings take place, conversations take place between those who are waiting their turn, balls advance in different combinations. In the end, of course, everything gets straightened out. People leave the party with the same person they arrived with, and, as a rule, nobody is offended. Of course, there have been times when some players have too much to drink and forget about the balls and just sort of take a gratuitous shot every once in a while while they put their primary energy into the flirtation or seduction that has moved, dangerously, beyond the fantasy level.

Some might feel that the sexuality of croquet is there only for those who are looking for it. This seems unlikely, as critics have been asking questions about the implications of playing croquet in mixed company since the late nineteenth century. In a game of bridge you might trump someone's trick, but in croquet you might be bending over in front of someone of the opposite sex at very close quarters.

○

There *is* a difference. Still, it is not as much a matter of actual physical positioning and real stimulation as it is of fantasy. Marketing campaigns would not be based on croquet if there were not more to this than meets the eye. Even the "romance" and "passion" potential in being taken through a wicket against your will brings a kind of tawdry provocativeness to the game. The innocent but flirtatious "What are you going to do with/to me?" questions that ring across a good social game provide a wonderfully enticing flavor and make of croquet a rich mélange of ménages.

O

Sex and croquet. Going all the way through wickets. None of the *demi-vierge* sort of stuff. Separation. Anticipation. Preparation. Coming together. Flirtation. Partnerships. Even ball-swapping. Combinations and variations. Sex and croquet: *Believe* it!

8

What Else Is at Stake?

Croquet has a wonderful richness, a festive and verdant vigor that has been expressed in a great many ways. The game has an emerging and growing following of young couples and an ongoing following of older couples. Croquet has been vilified as immoral and glorified as a game that brings equality to the sexes. It has been celebrated in song and captured colorfully in art. From Phoenix to Palm Beach, the home of the United States Croquet Association, from Santa Rosa to Newport, croquet's popularity is in rapid ascendancy once again. On both new and established courts in various places around the world, people of all ages and from all socio-economic strata are flocking every day to this maddeningly addictive and compellingly attractive game.

Some people play in the shadow of their BMW and others their old jalopy. Some play in New England college matches until the snow has fallen. A hundred and thirty years ago they played it happily in

In the nineteenth century croquet was played at the Bradley home in Old Siam in full formal dress despite high tropical temperatures and humidity. Photograph from the 1850s. *Courtesy: William Bradley Family Collection.*

Old Siam, and today it is played more in Australia than anywhere in the world. On the assumption that knowing more about a game makes it more interesting to play, I offer a few further perspectives, some curiosities, some notions and facts, by inviting you to travel through the following side wickets to discover just what else is at stake in this game.

Croquet in Art: The Winslow Homer Paintings

David Park Curry's wonderful book on Winslow Homer's croquet paintings is a gold mine of interesting information not only on croquet but on the history of its voyage in art. Curry's book was written in conjunction with a special Yale-based traveling exhibition in 1984 that, for the first time, brought together in one place Homer's five famous croquet oil paintings along with other drawings. While Curry cites various other paintings by other artists who also addressed croquet, such as Manet and Tissot, none seemed to "get into" the subject as fully as Homer, as was his wont when his enthusiasm ran high (consider, as a parallel, the wonderful set of watercolors he did in the Adirondacks; like the croquet paintings, they also were the subject of a special show at the Yale Art Gallery, in 1986).

In the croquet paintings, Homer displayed his usual special strengths in color and light, and his composition elements are strong. He also showed that he understood the game and its social customs, its attire and etiquette, as for example in the croquet scene presented here. In this painting, which hangs in the Art Institute of Chicago, a rather dapper gentleman bends down to assist a woman getting ready to take her croquet shot. As Curry points out, this depiction of men in rather subservient positions in croquet games, and usually with women outnumbering men in the overall composition, was typical of Homer and others. It was a way of downplaying the more aggressive, masculine side of the game, especially as it was being played by both sexes together. If men and women were to share an athletic outdoors for the first time, it would have to be only in the politest of ways, and of course one assumes that this relegation of men to a more passive role could only, in time, frustrate and in fact stimulate the appetite for a more adventurous approach.

The women in Homer's paintings are correctly dressed and stand carefully, a hand adjusting a bonnet or waiting in a genteel way to lift the skirt just ever so slightly to get the foot out from under. Other artists were more daring in illustrating the sensual side of the game, but none rivaled Homer in addressing the subject in art in a comprehensive way, with five major paintings all true to the fashion and decorum of the Victorian era.

The 1866 painting included here, interestingly enough, brings men and women together on a well-maintained lawn in an extremely verdant setting, just as in the Revlon Croquet advertisement, but the

Note that this fellow is pretty close to getting a good glimpse of an ankle! One of Winslow Homer's famous nineteenth-century croquet paintings ("The Croquet Game," 1866). *Courtesy: The Art Institute of Chicago.*

women are hardly recognizable as being cut from the same cloth. With one exception—the colors they wear play off the colors of the game, and in many ways, though the balls, mallets, and stakes together hardly constitute a critical mass of color, they jump forward because of the heavy greenness of the background. In this sense croquet makes a perfect vehicle for an artist. Because the overall amount of color is so small, you can't miss it. From the ribbon on a bonnet to the colors on the distant stake, each splash of color seems vivid and bold. The wood engraving included here, "Summer in the Country," was completed by Homer in 1869 and stands as a wonderful reminder of the social, carefree experience croquet represented to women as they began to take up the game so enthusiastically on both sides of the Atlantic. In any case, while croquet has not been presented in art very often, with many depictions both past and present assigned to merchandising croquet sets and other products, Homer's croquet paintings form a rare and wonderful example of social art history and stand as a wonderful tribute to a game that is still evolving.

Various minor artists did renditions of croquet in engravings and drawings, particularly for magazines, and, of course, the manufacturers of croquet sets used art to "sell" their wares. Today much of the depiction of croquet and equipment relies on photography.

"Summer in the Country"—Winslow Homer wood engraving, 1869. *Courtesy: The Bowdoin College Museum of Art.*

Croquet in Literature:
The Wicket Pages of History

The Croquet Player by H. G. Wells

That croquet has not always been treated in the most favorable light is apparent even more satirically in a novella entitled *The Croquet Player* written by H. G. Wells in 1936. With the threat of Nazi power growing daily, Wells takes his English countrymen to task by creating as the narrator of a moralistic "fable," a rich, idle, upper-class Englishman whose principal pastime is playing croquet: He daily plays croquet before noon, again in the afternoon, has dinner at eight, followed by bridge. Occasionally he pursues archery (he and his clinging aunt are both good at the "long bow"), but croquet is his thing. When he reads the daily paper, he is, he admits, vaguely aware that there is some other news in the air, but he mostly reads the pages about tennis and croquet.

As the quintessential croquet player, the narrator is drawn in harsh, satiric ways. He asserts that it takes great discipline and balance to be a good croquet player. He brags that he can make a croquet ball move pretty much like a trained animal. Never mind, he says, that he is considered effeminate, silly, and "soft" by some, he's not concerned. He was born after World War I and has been brought up in a sheltered, amiable sort of way. He is concerned that his self-satisfied world may be threatened in some way, and he prefers not to know more than that. When, at the end of the story, he is finally invited (challenged, really) point-blank to realize that "civilization" is changing and no longer the same, that steel and power are replacing the cushy, older social structure, he labels this change as just a lot of silly "apocalyptic stuff" and says, twice, that he just can't get involved. Though the world may be about to fall apart, though brute, uncivilized human nature may be resurfacing from the Stone Age, the most important thing right now is for him to leave in time to meet his aunt for a game of croquet—scheduled for half-past twelve.

That Wells chose to center his exhortation for the British (and the world) to wake up to the sinister forces threatening the very fabric of life and the future of mankind in a deprecating portrait of a croquet

In *Alice in Wonderland*, artist Sir
John Tenniel captured the difficulty of using flamingos as mallets
and hedgehogs as balls.

player, demonstrates the degree to which croquet and polite "civilization" had become synonymous in the popular culture. Croquet-
bashing in literature is not unique to Wells.

Alice Plays Croquet with the Queen of Hearts

In Lewis Carroll's *Alice's Adventures in Wonderland*, Alice is invited to
play a game of croquet with the domineering and emasculating Queen
of Hearts on the Queen's special croquet court. It is not like any
croquet court Alice has ever seen. Flamingos are used as mallets,
hedgehogs as balls, and weak-spined sheepish male cards bend over
to serve as wickets. Alice quickly sees that it is a very difficult game
as everyone begins playing at once—not waiting for turns—and *ar-
guing*.

Amid the pandemonium, Alice looks up and finds the Cheshire

O

Cat and begins to comment on how confusing the game is. The arriving King finds the cat impertinent, and Alice decides to return to the game. However, her mallet (flamingo) has flown off to the other side of the garden. She retrieves it and prepares to play, only to find that her hedgehog, which already had disappeared, was still off fighting with another hedgehog. At this point Alice is called upon to settle a dispute about whether or not the Cheshire Cat's head should be cut off. Soon the cat's head simply magically disappears, then the cat and the King and the executioner go charging around looking for it while the others return to the game.

Alice's misadventures on the Queen's croquet court are a wonderful commentary on the controversial nature of the game. Then, as now, the game inspires different opinions. Then, as now, people *argue* over the rules, over whose turn it is, and then, as now, people play out of turn! Carroll's fantasy underscores the increasingly accepted view that croquet is a game for all; the Queen is unable to capitalize on her position of clout and is instead made to appear foolish as she runs around saying "Off with their heads," her only way to be the superior player. The appearance of the grinning Cheshire Cat punctuates perfectly the smugness people can feel about the game, especially if they truly believe themselves superior to everyone else. Alice's game with the Queen of Hearts brings home forcefully the need to keep a healthy sense of humor about the game.

Death on the Croquet Court

If actually murdering someone on the croquet court is something you have long-harbored fantasies about (especially when playing against that pain-in-the-ass Fred), you will want to *rush* right out and read a very "wicket" and wonderful who-done-it by the British mystery writer, crime-book critic, and creator of Inspector Ghote, H.F.R. Keating. In his aptly named mystery, *A Rush on the Ultimate*, a group of croquet enthusiasts arrive (one's encased mallet is at first taken for an oboe) for an annual early September croquet tournament on the grounds of an English boarding school for boys.

MURDER BY MALLET

"Has anybody seen the paper?" he said. "I'd like to know what's happening in Africa. It's a nasty situation they've got there."

Michael Goohart handed him the paper.

"It seems to be pretty quiet still, thank goodness," he said.

"It isn't," said Leonard, "the very early news had more than the papers. There's been a lot of rioting."

"Oh, this violence," said Cicely, "I can't understand it."

"Rosalynn," said Irene, "draw the curtains. How often have I told you?"

"Sorry, madam," Rosalynn said. "I start in here before it's light outside and I kind of forget."

"That's all right, my dear, but draw them now."

Rosalynn went across to the window and reaching up as high as she could swished back the heavy blue curtains.

"Madam," she said.

Everyone turned to look at her.

The two syllables conveying simply horror.

Rosalynn jerked her head towards the windows. They all stepped forward to look.

Humphrey Boddershaw was lying face downwards on the croquet court. His shining bald skull had an ugly bloody broken patch in its absolute center. He could not have been alive. A blood-stained croquet mallet lay near him.

—from *A Rush on the Ultimate*, H.F.R. Keating

127

o

This September, however, the host of their group, headmaster Humphrey Boddershaw, is done in by a mallet. His bloodied bald pate is even comically foreshadowed by being splattered with an errant mulberry (deep red juice runs down over his eyes, an ear, and the nape of his neck!) when a storm interrupts the game the day before the murder. The novel offers a diverse cast of would-be mallet-wielding suspects, ranging from a former school groundskeeper recently escaped from prison and now hiding with the help of a serving girl in the shed where cricket bats are stored, to those who have an interest in shares of stocks, to an Australian just learning the game but who quickly becomes determined to solve the mystery.

Much of the suspense arises on the croquet court itself as different shots are intermingled with cat-and-mouse dialogue around a variety of motives and clues; the reader rules various suspects in and out as balls *clack* and, on occasion, bounce back from a hoop. The suspense builds in a final nerve-jarring game of croquet that leads to the denouement. Throughout the course of the mystery the reader is given a wonderful commentary on croquet and croquet players. One falsely suspected woman admits lying, for example, but explains: "What else could I do? I simply had to say something. I couldn't bear it a minute longer. I wasn't going to put up with it: the thought that one of us—a croquet player—had done a thing like that. It was unendurable, utterly unendurable."

In this excellent tale, we are allowed, even encouraged, to think about the way in which croquet only barely conceals some of our real killer instincts. It's a very different slant from H. G. Wells, but surely in the tradition of the Queen of Hearts!

Croquet and Fashion

There are certain occasions where there's a lot to be said about knowing what to wear. A croquet game is probably not one of them.

That's not to say that there is not a lot *being* said. In fact, there are some highly creative ideas centered around croquet clothing, par-

California designer Karen Thompson is in the lead in developing new varieties of "croquet whites" for those on the contemporary croquet fashion frontier. *Photograph © Sarah Puckitt.*

ticularly among some exciting designers in California. I talked with one of them, Karen Thompson, whose work is very dynamic.

You can play croquet in shirtsleeves (a T-shirt even) or in a classic white linen suit with a carefully selected oversize jacket. You don't just *play* croquet, you *wear* it. Croquet clothing can be as varied as the game itself, with all of the different levels of perception and skill being replicated through expressions of taste. Because croquet is a game, after all, as well as a sport, it can easily take on some of the fun of Halloween. It's a dress-up activity, even if you decide to dress down.

Most people who really *play* croquet (you know, seriously), have their "croquet whites," and to the extent that there is a standard, this is it. For instance, a stroll through New York's Central Park on a breezy Sunday afternoon finds croquet players (men and women) in baggy white pants, white shirts, off-white cable sweaters (baggy, of course, and often with a stripe or two around the v-neck), and white tennis shoes. COMFORT—but taste!

o

Some people, of course, think croquet is so boring that you have to at least put some excitement into the outing by doing something special with clothes. This can work. In fact I would recommend it. On the other hand, not too long ago an American couple visiting England was invited to the home of a couple they had met by chance. When they arrived, the English couple appeared—mallets in hand—stark naked.

There are, as you might guess, quite a range of croquet fashion choices between Napa Valley haute couture and nudity. Fashion, of course, means accessories, and over the years we have seen the rise and fall of such things as fans, muffs, boas, aprons, you name it. Even skirts have had their variety, with such entries as umbrella, bell, empire, grannie, yoke, and (my favorite) the tight-fitting eel (hard to line up on a wicket in that one though).

Fashion reflects ideas, and in a democratic society, when there are lots of ideas out there, fashion choices become abundant. The bustle which was first "out" in 1690 or so came roaring back in the nineteenth century. Embroidery became extravagant, compared at times to the metalwork on suits of armor. Hats got small, waists higher, and skirts broader—the so-called isoceles triangle look (seriously). By the turn of the century, knickerbockers, long popular with men, were entering women's wardrobes by way of attire for biking.

In 1870 a man might have worn a short-brimmed, rounded hat, a large-checked sport jacket (three buttons, and, by golly, all *buttoned*) as he set out on the croquet court, while his lady friend would have a long, grass-dusting, wide-bottomed skirt. In tennis she would have folded and hooked up some of her skirt at the front and used concealed elastic to keep the back part behind her—but that was for a game which required, you know, *movement*. She wouldn't have to

O

Taking a good clean shot without letting your bonnet slip off must be a sign of something, though it's not clear precisely what in this photograph taken on the Isle of Wight, 1910. *Courtesy: New York Public Library Picture Collection.*

worry about the molasses-like moves we've been learning about.

In England in the 1890s women went back to much of the "look" of the 1830s—their gowns coming tight in the bodice and narrow at the waist—with one exception: The upper arms were blown out, full and puffy, leading to the so-called "leg-of-mutton" look. Maybe they wanted to psych out their opponents with just a touch of threat in a supposed muscular upper arm. By the 1930s women were dressing like hour-glasses (albeit with stacked-up hair, flowers, jeweled combs, and topped with wide-brimmed promenade hats), and men looked like would-be ballet dancers hiding behind hunting coats, their own upper arms billowingly enlarged.

Croquet has seen a lot of "looks" come and go, and just as the

O

game itself has been around and in a state of change for six hundred years, one can only guess that croquet clothing will also be changing and being regarded differently. The current trend-setting styles in California are wonderful and what goes over in Palm Beach goes over in a lot of places. But I would guess that other new looks will come along.

There are a lot of different opinions today, but there is no base line. You can dress up. You can wear shorts. You can be cool, or you can be scruffy. In this regard, croquet has it all over other sports. I mean football and baseball, for example, have *uniforms*. You could not just enter a wrestling ring wearing any old thing; the crowd would expect you to appear in something between a jock-strap and a torn Turkish towel—and for the gals, well, long hair is pretty necessary (you know, for all the flipping and pulling activities). But in croquet you can wear what you want. I mean somebody might notice what you are wearing, but then again, since it's such a sleepy-time thing (on the surface only), it's not real likely—unless it's understood at the outset (invitation level) that everyone is going to "dress up" or "dress down." In these instances it becomes a lot of fun. When everyone comes in "croquet whites" the total effect is terrific.

Just remember: You can be a tease in your chemise, a jock in a frock, wear a modesty piece over your décolletage (it doesn't mean that you *graduated* from college, only that you *attended*), anything, in fact, you have the stomach for. Fashion and croquet go together like, well, tea and crumpets. Whether Napa Valley high fashion or back-yard cut-offs is your thing, by putting some hustle in your bustle you can bring some real life onto the croquet scene.

Final tips: Shrink what's too big, give away what's too small, don't opt for multiple zippers or contrasting-color top-stitching. Whether you like to drip-dry or tumble dry, cool iron, hot iron, or dry-clean only, there are plenty of choices. Above all, to avoid being a court jester in polyester or a buffoon in pantaloons, and to avoid a trip to Hong Kong for a well-tailored English wool suit (of 10–14 ounce weight for fall/winter), just put you and your clothes into the right croquet cycle—the gentle cycle—and that's all that's needed to be wicketly fashionable.

Croquet and Psychology: *Can Croquet Beat Psychotherapy?*

A 1987 *Wall Street Journal* article noted that more and more Americans who participate in "hard" aerobic sports become so compulsive and goal-oriented that they must seek counseling to undo some of the effects of the good they are doing. As I am a daily runner, I know the addiction of which I speak, and one must fight all the time to keep aerobic exercise in proper perspective. We are not, despite our yearnings, all cut out to be Olympic athletes.

According to the article, "Mind Games: Weekend Athletes Seek Help From Sports Psychology," some one thousand "doctoral-level psychologists" are busily treating patients for both real and potentially psychosomatic sports injuries. This statistic compels one to reflect again on the nature of the relationship between sports and leisure time.

Sports began only when people were first able to pause and do something besides concentrate on surviving. Such early sports as wrestling and archery, in fact, evolved from such survival-related activities as fighting and hunting. Throughout history, people have turned to sports for good mental health. The problem, as underscored by the growing need for counseling, is that too many people are so excessively gung-ho about becoming aerobically more fit that they are becoming mentally less fit. Obviously this is not true of everyone, and certainly not for millions of relatively satisfied joggers, bikers, workout lovers, and so forth. Still, croquet's growing popularity, and indeed the emerging popularity of a variety of *less* physically de-manding sports, may well also be a measure of support for the notion that we have reached the point where we must pull back a bit from demanding aerobic exercise and take on a gentle game of croquet where you can be competitive, compulsive, addicted . . . and yet not subject yourself either to brain-chemical addiction or physical injury. And you can buy a croquet set for the price of a therapy session—as many people obviously are, from Napa Valley to Lake George.

Drinks and Food: Croquet Refreshments

Given the fact that even if you have "graduated," as some express it, from backyard croquet to competitive six-wicket American croquet ("the" game, some say; the "real game," others say; "a" game, still others say), there are going to be times when you are invited over, or when you invite someone else over, simply for a "fun game of croquet"—of one kind or another. Question is: What to serve?

Bear in mind that croquet can be pretty slow and people can have a lot of time on their hands, and probably not *all* of it can be absorbed easily through conversation, flirtation, and so forth. Refreshments should be provided. If you really want to make a big impact, hire a bartender (ask him to wear a white shirt, a black bow tie, and black trousers) and let people simply order mixed drinks. This is fine so long as you have no serious interest in having a good game but instead are simply using the idea of coming over for a game of croquet as a "tice" to get friends heading in your direction. The idea works well, in fact, if you are indebted to some people and feel you should have them back but also feel you have absolutely *nothing* to talk about. It's amazing how much yardage you can get by asking who's shot it is, who's dead on whom, why are you doing this to me, what should I/he/she do next? You can probably get through several hours this way and never be pressed for something "real" to talk about, and if you are served drinks, well, that makes it all flow even more easily.

Gin and tonics, white wine, white wine spritzers, cold beer and ice—are probably the most popular drinks to have with croquet. Champagne in champagne glasses makes for a wonderful party; you can begin this way and then let people switch to white wine. And remember, every once in a while a player really will be taking a turn and will need to be able to put a glass down, so having some small outdoor tables around the edges of the court is a good idea. Why

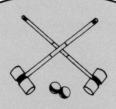

CHRISTOPHER'S FAVORITE
CROQUET DRINK

I am always amazed when I go to a Polynesian restaurant and find the first half of the menu sensuously describing exotic drinks, usually blending fruit juices and rum, but sometimes strutting out into more dangerous territory with various combinations of vodka and liqueurs.

Anyway, I can't begin to compete with all of that. A "lemon lily" is one especially fine drink I like to serve: Make iced decaffeinated coffee, add just a touch of milk, a bit of sugar, and stick a full circular slice of lemon on the rim of the glass. It's a light and wonderful combination and lacks alcohol, which means you can keep abreast of developments. For Steve and Wendy, however, you can add a lot of vodka to the lemon lily and, without changing its innocuous name, turn it into a veritable mine whose explosive punch will be felt only just before it's too late. In general, I would tend to serve it to Steve first, let him get out of control, watch Wendy worry briefly—until the drink you've prepared for her but served twenty minutes later hits her right in the old mallet and she goes belly-up too! It might seem cruel to do this, but then I can remember being done in with a "light" (he said) gin and tonic (several, actually) that Steve foisted on me. So my favorite way to go is to use the old lemon lily to pollute them but keep myself squeaky clean for the big win.

O

ruin your own fun by watching everyone place a glass on the lawn and knock it over, apologize, fill it up, and do it again?

Heavy food is out because people will be standing most of the time. Plates of hors d'oeuvres passed every so often should be fine. If, as with H. G. Wells's croquet player, the game is either at noon (a new idea for a "nooner") or before dinner, it is more than likely that some sort of food will be needed. Being practical, you might even prepare sandwiches ahead (trimming the crusts makes them a big deal) so that everyone will actually have drinks and food as part of the "fun game of croquet," and will therefore not need to be called to dinner after the game. After all, given the nasty behavior of Steve and Wendy, the last thing you want to do is *feed* them afterward! Poison, yes, food, no.

If you do go for a real dinner party following the game, make it a barbecue/cookout or a buffet-type affair. I favor the latter, as trying to cook, much less tend a fire, and also enjoy the game can be a real pain: More than once a cookout dinner has been ruined in the final half hour of a croquet game. In general it is easiest to serve a pre-prepared cold buffet supper, for then everyone can go through a line when he wants to, and the diehards who want to keep playing can get around to the food later on, without anyone having to worry about its being "ready." In any case, try to discourage people from getting food on the lawn, from setting drinks down on the lawn, and above all, from eating while trying to take a turn. Those one-handed strokes (the other with glass or sandwich) are usually terrible. Let the refreshments complement the game, not dominate it.

The Future of Croquet

One of the more curious aspects of croquet (and by now it should be apparent that there are many!) is that it has had trouble shaking off its image as a game for the upper class. Even though it is now played happily in different ways by many different peoples, there are still some who persist in thinking about "real" croquet. While one should take pride in being a good player and in developing one's skills to full potential (if that is what one wants), it is important to bear in mind that you go into croquet with the deck a bit loaded, for there simply are some croquet players who think a bit possessively about the sport, though they deny it. One thinks of the satirized view of W. S. Gilbert in his operetta, *Ruddigore I*: "You've no idea what a poor opinion I have of myself—and how little I deserve it."

Here are two questions I was asked in the course of writing this book: "Have you talked with _____ ? She/he really knows a lot about *real* croquet." I said that I had not, though I knew of her or him and of her or his contributions to the development of the sport, and that I hoped to talk with her or him. Inside, though, I was still having trouble dealing with "real" croquet, because I guess I like all the "false" ones too. The more loaded question was simply "Are you a *player*?" I said that yes, I played croquet, but no, I was not a professional, tournament player, but rather a writer who enjoyed playing the game, like millions of other people. A question like that unfortunately sets in motion the old problems croquet has had in shaking off its heritage as a game for the idle rich, the notion that Wells so forcefully attacked in his *Croquet Player*.

The largest manufacturer of croquet equipment, and the only one in this country, Forster of Maine, recently provided me with very helpful literature about their various sets. They have twelve lines of croquet sets, for people interested in playing croquet at a variety of levels of intensity, skill, competitiveness, and so forth. Forster knows well that there is a need for a large variety, as is the case with most sports. That the United States Croquet Association approves only their "Challenge" set for official play is perfectly fine, but this does not have any bearing on the sets that thousands of others should select for play in their own yards.

In other words, croquet is like any other game. It can be played different ways and with different versions of equipment. The main purpose of the game is to have a good time, and while it is wonderful to dress up in the latest croquet fashion, have some champagne, and use the best equipment, it is also good to remind ourselves that this is all supposed to be *fun*.

In all likelihood, it will be a long time before croquet completely shakes off its earlier elitist stereotypes, but as other colleges besides those of New England fame begin to play competitively, and as more public courts are installed in different municipalities, eventually croquet will be understood as a wonderfully democratic, accessible, low-cost sport for everyone. To the extent that we can bring all of this about sooner, so much the better. In the meantime, let everyone have true respect for everyone else's style, dress, equipment, and, by the same token, let those who make fun of the stylish, competitive players—the connoisseurs of the game—bear in mind that much of the game's recent popularity is due to the efforts of these same people. The leadership provided by those more deeply "into" the game has been entirely beneficial to the development of the sport. Other developments are under way, from construction of courts to increased publication of books, magazines, and articles.

It might be useful to recall Charles Dickens's comment, in *The Pickwick Papers* : "I am delighted to view any sport that may be safely engaged in." Or perhaps turn to Shakespeare's lines from *The Comedy of Errors*: "When the sunne shines, let foolish gnates make sport."

Croquet brings everyone in the family together, as in this photograph taken in 1905. The older man on the left is Horatio Stonier; the ladies in the second row, the fourth and fifth from the left, are his daughters Gertrude and Eliza, while son Edmond mysteriously holds a tennis racket on the far right. There's at least one in every family! *From the Patricia Dubin Family Collection.*

Glossary

Alive: When you are "alive" on a ball, you can hit it and thereby earn two additional strokes. In American croquet you must pass through a wicket to become "alive" on a ball you have already hit; until you clear a wicket, you are "dead" on it. Expressed differently, you cannot hit the same ball twice and earn extra strokes until you have cleared a wicket. In British croquet, by contrast, you are "alive" on all balls at the start of each turn. If you are really dead on a ball and presume to play as if you are *alive* on it, you incur a penalty—which is administered only if you are caught in time, namely, before the next player has taken a turn. When each of two players are playing two balls, as in tournament games, you need to be very careful to remember which balls are dead on which.

Association croquet: The name given to the British six-wicket version of croquet; so-named after the English Croquet Association.

Aunt Emma: Name given to a boring, unadventurous, conservative player who usually takes no chances and simply tries to progress cautiously from one wicket to the next.

Ball-in-hand: A ball literally picked up by hand after it has either been hit or knocked out of bounds; it is then moved to where it should be placed. Following a roquet, you can pick up your ball and place it, for example, flush against the other ball. Note that in British croquet you can pick up a wired ball and move it, whereas in American croquet you cannot touch it.

Bisque: A shot "taken over" from where it was first played; bisques are usually offered to players who are not as strong, thereby giving them a better chance to compete. A bisque is like a handicap stroke in golf. In some games the player can exercise his right to take the bisque at any time, in others, only under certain circumstances. In British croquet, a standard bisque can be taken whenever the player wishes.

Break: Used to keep your turn going as long as possible, a break results when you are able to run through a series of wickets by making use of another ball (known as a *two-ball break*), two other balls (*three-ball break*), or three other balls (*four-ball break*). A break is essentially at the heart of croquet strategy because you are using your skill and wits to take advantage of the presence of other balls in order to advance your ball through the wickets faster than anyone else. Sometimes a player can run the whole course in his turn by succeeding in making breaks of various kinds (see discussions of strategies in chapter 5).

Break down: Just as your car comes to a halt, so do you: the end of your turn for failing to make a shot or by incurring a penalty.

Cannon shot: Generally used to describe a croquet stroke that makes a roquet.

Cleaning (and **Clearing**): Giving your dead ball new life by going through a wicket (in American croquet only; in British croquet, you have "cleaned yourself" and you are alive on all balls as soon as you begin your next turn). A "clean" ball is one, therefore, that has passed through a wicket and not yet hit another ball. Thankfully, there is no such opposite form (that is, dirty ball).

O

Clips: In more formal play, these are placed on wickets to indicate where you are in the game; the clips are of the same colors as the balls. A clip goes on top of the wicket when you are to proceed through it in one direction (first time) and on the side of the wicket when you need to pass through it in the opposite (reverse) direction later on. Clips are generally used only in tournament play or by the easily confused.

Continuation stroke: When you make a roquet (hit another ball on which you are alive) and earn two strokes, the first of the two is known as a croquet stroke and the second as a *continuation stroke*. Some people also refer to the stroke earned when you pass through a wicket as a continuation stroke. In any event, you'll use it to *continue* your play.

Corner: To hit your ball or your partner's ball into one of the corners of the court as a safe hiding place; this is a defensive move, and anyone who is enticed to come after you (see *tice*) will hopefully miss and go out of bounds.

Croquet stroke: The stroke that follows making a roquet. You use it by placing your ball next to the ball you have hit (made the roquet on) and then hitting your ball in such a way as to move both balls. While you generally will move both balls, it is acceptable in basic backyard American croquet instead to place your ball a mallet head's length away from the ball you have hit and proceed to take both the *croquet stroke* and the continuation stroke. This is often a way to get ahead of the ball you have hit by at least one wicket.

Deadness: When your ball hits another ball (roquet), it is rewarded with two additional strokes, a croquet stroke and a continuation stroke. You are, however, now *dead* on the ball your ball hit until you pass through the next sequential wicket. After that you are again live on that particular ball. You can become dead on any number of balls, then pass through a wicket, and become live on all of them immediately. When making breaks it can become tricky to remember which balls you are alive on and which dead on; to assist memory in this process, in tournament play a *deadness board* is often used.

Drive shot: The shot you make when you strike your ball very directly; your ball usually goes about one-third as far as the ball you hit. You hit the other ball straight and hard with a level swing in this frequently used croquet stroke.

Footing the ball: Placing your foot on your own ball, which you strike but still hold in place so that the impact of the strike is felt only on the adjacent ball, which you are sending; not permitted in British croquet but used with great frequency (and exhilaration) in informal American games and permitted in American croquet.

Hoop: The English word used instead of *wicket* and now synonymous with it. The term derives from the early, larger hoops through which balls were knocked in the first version of the game as played in France in the thirteenth century.

Jaws: Not of the great whites, but of the little whites, that is, the mouthlike opening between the sides ("uprights") of the wicket; this is a quintessential example of how the language of croquet tries to bring an element of excitement and physical confrontation into the game. Dangerous as "jaws" sounds, don't get uptight about uprights.

Jump shot: You chop down at your ball in such a way as to force it to jump up off the ground. The *jump shot* is primarily used to jump over a ball that is wicketed; you want to jump over the opponent's ball, rather than take it through the wicket, whereas you might make a *half-jump shot* to climb partway up your partner's ball that might be wicketed, with the result that while you are going over it, the partner's ball will also advance through the wicket. You can even try to jump over the stake, but it is hard and, unlike Jack and his candlestick, you have to be not only nimble and quick but very strong!

Laying a break: As in pool or billiards game, you *lay a break* to send balls in a way that they will be in a position to be used advantageously. Your concern is to leave the balls in optimally helpful positions and particularly to enable you to make breaks.

Leave: Where the balls are left after your turn.

Lower stake: In nine-wicket croquet where there are stakes at both ends of the court, the nearer (game opening) stake is the *lower* and the farther, opposite end (halfway point) is the *upper*.

Peel or **peel shot:** The shot that you make to hit a ball (not your own) through a wicket; as a rule, you *peel* your partner's ball through a wicket, though you might for strategic reasons decide to peel an opponent's ball through as well, usually to prepare for a new break, and particularly if the opponent ball would have had no difficulty going through the wicket on the next turn anyway. If you peel an opponent ball through a wicket, that does not earn that ball's player an extra stroke; it simply has cleared the wicket. The same holds true when you peel your partner's ball through a wicket. You can hit a ball, become dead on it, peel it through a wicket, then go through the wicket with your remaining stroke, be live on that ball again, and be in a position to use it more easily than if it had been left behind with the wicket between you as a possible obstruction. There can be a lot of (sex) appeal in all of this!

Pegging out: Hitting the final stake and going out of the game; your *pegging-out shot* is your final shot of the game. You are a rover ball from the time you pass through the final wicket up until the time you peg out. Note that you can hit your own rover ball into the stake or be hit into it by another ball, also a rover. Either way, you are completely out of the game.

Push: Leaving your mallet head "*pushed*" flush against your ball as you make a croquet shot; it is used in the beginning of a roll shot, and you are not supposed to speed up your push as you do it.

Roll or **roll shot:** You make a roll, as a croquet stroke, when you hit your ball and a second ball in such a way that they travel straight together in a full roll, to the same stopping point; by hitting your ball with a large sweeping motion, you can make it keep traveling just as the other ball you have hit is traveling. You can, alternatively, vary your rolls in such a way as to make your ball travel only half as far as the other ball (a *half roll*), and so forth. With practice you can make both balls stop at a certain distance. A *pass roll* results when you hit your ball in such a way as to make

Glossary

○

144

it keep traveling farther than the other ball. This is useful, for example, if you want to bring your ball and your partner's near a wicket but leave your ball closer to go through the wicket on the next stroke.

Roquet: The term used to describe successfully making one ball hit another ball.

Rover: A ball that has cleared all the wickets but not yet hit the stake to peg out. A *rover ball* is never dead but is instead live on all other balls. The rover can, as the name purposely suggests, rove from one ball to another and "hit on" anyone!

Rush or **rush shot:** This describes what happens when you make your ball hit another ball (roquet) to a particular spot. A *rush*, in effect, "rushes" the roqueted ball over to the place you want it to be, while you still have remaining the two extra strokes you have earned for making the roquet. In this sense, a rush can be used almost like a third stroke. When you "set" a rush, you are taking the shot preceding it, getting set to make the rush on it, which usually means that you are lining up on it. So, for example, if you have won a pair of additional strokes on a roquet off one ball, you can use one to set a rush and then actually rush a third ball. Such a strategy is not uncommon when playing a three-ball break. The course of the balls in a rush is known as the *rush line*. A *cut rush* sends both balls at particular angles on the rush, again with the desire to advance the roqueted ball to a particular spot.

Split shot: A very basic croquet stroke that moves both your ball (the only one you ever strike) *and* the adjacent ball in different directions. You set up the angle from which to strike your own ball to make it and the adjacent ball travel in particular directions by the same principles as a pool shot.

Stop shot: Describes the act of hitting your ball in a hard, upward, chopping stroke in order to make your ball move just a little (that is, stop) while the croqueted ball travels farther, depending on how hard you chop. Because you are swinging the face of your mallet upward, the heel of your mallet digs in and keeps the mallet from following through, thus softening the impact or momentum likely in your own ball and transferring the force through your ball primarily to the croqueted ball.

Strike: The word used to describe your "hitting" of your ball; you are, at this point, known as the *striker*.

Stroke: The deliberate movement of your mallet to move your ball; it cannot be accidental. Taking a stroke, in effect, begins your turn, and you gain an extra stroke for clearing a wicket or hitting the first stake (in nine-wicket croquet), and two additional strokes for hitting any other ball on which you are live. If you miss your ball, your turn is still over, except in a gentle and friendly game.

Take-off shot: The opposite of a stop shot; your ball "takes off" from the croqueted ball, which in turn stays where it is. The croqueted ball must move (visibly enough to prevent raging arguments), and you can make a *take-off shot* at almost right angles to the other ball, which for strategic purposes you want to keep right where it is.

Tice: From the word "entice," a *tice* shot is one in which you position your ball in such a way as to entice an opponent's ball to seek you out, with the hope that it will either miss you and thereby leave itself in a poor position or even go out of bounds. It is clearly a seductive strategy and has a come-and-get-me challenge that fits in with the undercurrents of courtship and romance discussed in text. A tice temporarily invests a croquet ball with the personality of a courtesan.

Wicket: The basic arch through which the ball passes. If you are *wicketed* you are caught in the wicket. You are considered through a wicket only if you can run your mallet down the side without having it touch your ball.

Wired: Your ball is *wired* if the wicket (or stake) is in the way of its being hit by another ball. It is not a ball that is supercharged but one that is, in fact, a bit out of it.